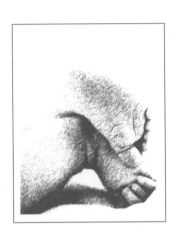

PRAYERS FOR
NEW
MOTHERS

by
Angela Thomas Guffey

Honor Books
Tulsa, Oklahoma

Second Printing

Prayers for New Mothers
ISBN 1-56292-776-0
Copyright © 2000 by Angela Thomas Guffey

Published by **Honor Books**
P.O. Box 55388
Tulsa, Oklahoma 74155

For
my parents,
Joe and Novie Thomas—

I will spend the rest of my life
trying to be like you.

Acknowledgments

If there is anything more challenging than writing a book while you're pregnant, it is writing a book after your fourth baby. Thankfully, I have not written alone. My whole family pulled together to let "Mommy" write.

I would like to say thank you to my husband, Paul, for his enduring confidence in me; thank you to my children, Taylor, Grayson, William and Anna Grace, for counting my prayers and celebrating my progress; thank you to my parents, Joe and Novie Thomas, for letting the children and I move in for a month so I could write. Thank you especially, Mama, for corralling the herd at the big house while I hid away in peace. You definitely had the harder job. I love you all more than I could ever say.

A special note of appreciation to my family and friends who encouraged me in these days: Craig and Kim Thomas, April and Amanda, Jonathan and Jodi Thomas, Ima Thomas, Jerry and Carlye Arnold, Nicole Johnson, Laura Johnson, and my church family at First Baptist Oviedo.

Thank you, Robert Wolgemuth and Jennifer Cortez for great literary representation; Rebecca Currington for kindly editing my sentence fragments; and Honor Books for the privilege of praying in print for new mothers like me.

My deepest gratitude to my Savior, Jesus Christ. His love is abundant, and His grace is always enough. I acknowledge my complete dependence upon Him and testify to His constant faithfulness to me. May He find pleasure in these prayers and use them for His glory.

INTRODUCTION

Being a new mother is perhaps the most blessed and the most tiring thing I have ever done in my life. Four times, the season of new baby has come to our home, each one incredibly wonderful and stressful and extraordinary. Each time I find myself praying aloud, "Lord, help me. Teach me how to love this baby well."

While I wrote these prayers during our first months with Anna Grace, I also drew from experiences with our other babies. Taylor was our first, and we prayed desperate first-baby prayers and tender awe-struck prayers over her. Grayson was next. We gave thanks for his life because of a difficult birth. We prayed for extra stamina when he didn't sleep through the night for fourteen months. And we prayed for his health when he had seizures that scared us senseless. Then came William—wild and wonderful William. We didn't know that our angel baby would turn into an adorable, extra-curious two-year-old who requires constant prayer for protection. As I write these words, I am wondering, *What is William doing?* The house has been unusually quiet for all of fifteen seconds, and I am worried.

It is a privilege to share my prayers with you. As you pray through your own season of new mothering, may our tender God hold you tight and love you long. If you will call out to Him, He will be faithful to come and abide. He will be your portion and your strength. He will be your delight and your rest. The child you hold in your arms proves again His great love for you.

Press on, my sister . . . pray in all things . . . and kiss that baby for me.

Angela Thomas Guffey

CONTENTS

Prayers

THE GIFT

OH, WONDERFUL LORD,

Today we brought home our gift. Awesome. Breathtaking. Stunning. Surely, she is the most amazing gift I have ever known. It is love at first sight, and I am consumed with pride. I am totally at peace. Finally, the one we have prayed for has safely arrived and come home.

The whole day has been dreamlike. A tiny new outfit just for the ride home. A proud daddy with a complicated car seat. Video and pictures and good-byes to the nurses. A car full of balloons and flowers and new baby things. Her first breath outside, the first breeze through her hair, her first ride in a mini-van. Our joy in introducing her to the whole family.

Now there is new life in our home. Someone lies in the cradle, sleeping as if she has always been here. She breathes and squirms like she's done it for years. We find great delight in just watching her sleep. Blankets and cloth diapers now scatter the house. Dirty baby clothes already need washing. This sleeping little bundle has quickly established her place in our home and our hearts.

Thank You, God, for answering our prayers. Thank You for this homecoming. Thank You for the gift of our child. I can look into the eyes of our gift and see my own reflection. I am so humbled. I never could have dreamed what this day would be like. I am a mother; she is my child; and we are home.

I bless You, God. I am happy and full of Your favor. Truly, You are an awesome God. In Jesus' name,

AMEN.

Behold, children are a gift of the LORD; The fruit of the womb is a reward.

—Psalm 127:3 NAS

13

WONDERFULLY MADE

O GOD,

This child You gave us is already so precious to me. She is Your creation, fearfully and wonderfully made. You deserve all my praise. I hold her against my tummy and cannot believe that she came from me. Although I tried, I could not imagine the magnificent work You were doing in the secret place of my womb.

Her skin is the softest I have ever touched—her fingers and toes, perfection. Her full head of hair swirls in a silly and wayward fashion. It must be pure silk just spun by an angel. Her big eyes with great eyelashes, her little bird mouth, her tightly clenched fists—I am intrigued by every part of her. Even the smell of her newness thrills me. I could linger forever at the nape of her neck, praying that I will never forget her fresh fragrance.

I am awestruck by Your creation. I want to shout from the highest place, in my loudest voice, "My God is Almighty, my God is miraculous." I hold her tightly, and I sing. I sing hymns. I sing lullabies. I just sing. I praise You for this child who has come and filled a place in my heart—a mommy place that was there all along and waiting for her.

I feel keenly aware that my life will never be the same. Yet I wouldn't go back for all the treasure in the world. How did I ever live without her? Thank You, sweet Lord, for the immeasurable gift of our baby. "Your works are wonderful, I know that full well." Hallelujah.

AMEN.

For you created my inmost being; you knit me together in my mother's womb. I praise you because I am fearfully and wonderfully made; your works are wonderful, I know that full well. My frame was not hidden from you when I was made in the secret place. When I was woven together in the depths of the earth, your eyes saw my unformed body.

—Psalm 139:13–16

A GOOD NAME

ALL-KNOWING GOD,

I cannot believe we brought our daughter home from the hospital without a name. Paul called the birth certificate office from my room and received a five-day extension. Our friends and family call every day and ask, "Does she have a name yet?"

This is ridiculous. The administrator said we can call in her name to the office anytime. I just wish we had one. I feel so frustrated. We brought all our other children home with a name.

We have had the nine months of pregnancy to consider this matter. Yet our family still doesn't feel peace or consensus. All the children want to call her Tessa because Tessa means fourth child.

I'm okay with Tessa but not totally sure. Paul likes Kristin, Christy, or Christine, but he says her name is totally my decision. He relinquished all rights to name selection at the ultrasound appointment, as he begged to find out the sex of our child. Although I reinstated his naming rights, he refuses to budge on the matter.

Lord, I think I really like the name Anna Grace. It means grace upon grace. Is that the name You intended? Is that what You already call her? We've all agreed that her middle name should be Nicole. Anna Grace Nicole. Is that it? It feels peaceful to say. It seems that we are joining You in naming our child. I believe that's her name.

Father, bless her. Bless this precious new person—Anna Grace Nicole. Make her name good—better than fine perfume. Thank You for the peace that You have given me through prayer. Thank You for a truly beautiful name for our beautiful daughter. In Jesus' name,

AMEN.

A good name is better than fine perfume.

—Ecclesiastes 7:1

AFTERSHOCKS

LORD,

If the earth moved on the day I gave birth, then today brings the rumblings of that big quake's aftershocks. Afterbirth pains. Why didn't I have this intense pain before? Why didn't somebody tell me it gets worse after each child? I prepared myself for the pain that comes with childbirth, but I wasn't ready for the tremendous pain of recovery. Agony. This is all pain with no glory—nothing wonderful waits at the end.

These waves of contractions feel like the final stages of labor all over again. Oh, for an at-home epidural kit! The heating pad and ibuprofen do little to soothe a contracting uterus. I resort to breathing techniques just to manage the intensity of the pain. And nursing—nursing makes it even worse. Lord, I'm undone by this pain. I'm frazzled. I'm crying. I desperately need Your comfort and healing.

I ask You to intervene. Please, Lord, quickly make these pains go away. Give me patience with recovery. My body has been through more than I can understand. Stitches, sore everything, a headache, and now these aftershocks. Yuck. I hadn't given much thought to these days. The goal was giving birth. Recovery sounded easy.

Lord, I know that these contractions will soon pass, but would You bring relief right now? Allow me some rest between the pains. Let me dream of my baby. I'd still do it all again for her. I love You. Thank You for meeting me in these difficult hours. I trust that relief will come soon. I pray expectantly in Your name.

AMEN.

Praise be to the God and Father of our Lord
Jesus Christ, the Father of compassion and
the God of all comfort, who comforts
us in all our troubles.

—2 Corinthians 1:3–4

SHE KNEW MY VOICE

DEAR SHEPHERD OF MINE,

The delivery room was busy, yet serene. And
then, out popped our pumpkin. She began with
just a few whimpers and quickly worked herself
into full-blown newborn baby wails. A quick exam
by the nurse didn't help matters. Our little one
was mad, and she wanted everyone to know it.

Finally, they brought her to me. We couldn't
even hear ourselves talk over her cries until I
whispered into her ear, "I love you." Suddenly,
her cries stopped. Her vocal expressions of fear
and anger immediately calmed at the sound of
my voice.

She knew my voice. I will never forget it. I will
forever remember how it felt to be the only

person in the room who could comfort my baby. Gratifying. Humbling. Awesome. At that moment, I knew I was her mother—and she was my child. A Scripture passage quickly came to mind, "His sheep follow him because they know his voice" (John 10:4).

What a privilege to shepherd this new lamb in our flock. She is innocent and pure and completely dependent on the voice she knows. Lord, I promise to speak gently to her and speak love into her life. I promise to attend to her needs and listen for her tender cries. I promise to look to You as my Shepherd and listen for Your voice. I promise to lead her according to Your direction and guide her where You lead.

She knew my voice. I delight in the wonder of it all. Thank You, Jesus, thank You. May I always know the voice of my Father. In Your precious name,

AMEN.

The sheep listen to his voice. He calls his own sheep by name and leads them out. When he has brought out all his own, he goes on ahead of them, and his sheep follow him because they know his voice. But they will never follow a stranger; in fact, they will run away from him because they do not recognize a stranger's voice.

—John 10:3–5

JAUNDICE

FATHER,

We ventured to the doctor for a two-day check-up yesterday. By the time we arrived, Anna Grace appeared extremely yellow. A heel prick and some test results confirmed jaundice. A home-health care nurse visited last night and swiftly turned our house into a makeshift pediatric unit.

Now Anna Grace lies wrapped in a blanket of lights and plugged into a special machine. She radiates like a neon-green glowworm. A chart must log her temperature, each diaper change, and every feeding.

Her heel was stuck again for the fourth time in her first two days of life. Every twelve hours, blood must be taken. And the nurse thinks we'll need to do this for a week. I expected some adjustment in her first days, but this is over the top.

Lord, help me to know how to comfort my daughter. Let us begin to bond even with a glowing thick pad of lights between us. Give my postpartum body enough energy to plow through these next few days. We are forced to stay home so she can be plugged in. That is good—for all of us.

So very early, I must learn to trust You to care for Anna Grace. I do. She belongs to You, but a gift to us and temporarily a beautiful shade of yellow. Thank You for her and thank You for the neon glow in her bassinet that heals her brand new body. Quickly restore pink to her precious newborn skin. I will comfort her with the comfort You give to me. In Your strong name, I pray.

AMEN.

As a mother comforts her child,
so will I comfort you.

—Isaiah 66:13

MY MOTHER

OH, GOD,

Thank You. Thank You for my mother. I never fully understood how incredible she really is until the birth of my first child. With this birth, my esteem for her is renewed. My respect for her grows daily. She truly embodies the truth of Proverbs 31—a woman of great character, noble and praiseworthy and good.

My mother is a source of great strength. Her presence always brings calm and assurance. With each new baby, she quietly comes and takes her place in our home. She brings handmade gowns and blankets that will become family treasures. She cooks and cleans and irons. She holds everything together while I fall apart. She has given each of our children his or her first bath. Even now, I hear her humming a lullaby, and I smell the beginnings of supper on the stove. It is so peaceful to rest in the love of my mother.

Lord, her legacy is one which I long to pass on as well. Although I am at the start of motherhood, I desire more than anything to give my children the same motherly love that I have known. I feel completely inadequate, yet wholly committed. Continue to teach me through Mama how to love my babies well.

Please bless her. Give her happiness beyond measure. Reward her many times over for each sacrifice she has made. Let her know that she is loved and adored by her children. Thank You, God, for giving me a mother to love. Give us many more years to walk together. From the tender heart of Your daughter and hers, I gratefully pray in Your name.

AMEN.

A wife of noble character who can find? . . . Her children arise and call her blessed; her husband also, and he praises her: "Many women do noble things, but you surpass them all."

—Proverbs 31:10,28–29

MOMMY SINGS THE BLUES

OH, LORD MY GOD,

Postpartum blues ambush my joy. Hormones fluctuate. Tears puddle. I just feel sad. My mind keeps telling me I'm thrilled. I feel myself smiling politely. But my heart is cloudy and overcast.

I have read about postpartum depression but hoped I would be an exception. I'm not. I feel empty and numb. Maybe this is more than hormones. Perhaps my indifferent heart comes from weaving a great big ending with an even bigger beginning. I am overwhelmed. A huge event, yet the anticlimax of finally having our baby. The elation of holding our child, yet the exhaustion. Visitors and gifts. Night sweats and chills. A long look in a full-length mirror. There's a lot going on within me. Maybe my heart cannot embrace the spectrum of emotion, so it has shut down for a while.

A numb heart paralyzes all of me. It's even hard to fake it. Maybe I can sleep this off. Maybe it will just drift away. I'm weepy but know there's every reason to rejoice. Lord, let this all pass quickly. Restore bright days and my hope for the future. Wipe these tears away, and give my husband patience. How could he possibly understand what I cannot begin to describe? This must be one of those "girl things" that even I don't understand.

I will trust You, and I will trust that one morning very soon, rejoicing will replace my weeping. Actually, tomorrow would be great because weepiness doesn't become me. Thank You for listening. Thank You for not being shocked by my weakness. Thank You for the comfort You already bring. I love You.

AMEN.

Weeping may remain for a night, but rejoicing comes in the morning.

—Psalm 30:5

NURSING

LORD,

I love nursing my baby, and I love being forced to sit still and look at Anna Grace every few hours. I love being needed—no, demanded. Her sweet little cries beckon Mommy, and no one else will do. It's miraculous and intimate and peaceful. The baby is awesome. She knows exactly where to turn her head and how to open her mouth. I marvel that she can be satisfied through me.

Still, Lord, there are many reasons to pray. My breasts are engorged and incredibly sore. I feel like I'm going to bite right through my lip when she latches on. Everyone says it will get better, and so I ask You to let me nurse without pain. Give me a persevering heart. I know it will get easier. I just need to hang on.

I also trust You to nourish my baby. I still don't know whether to nurse on demand or try to get us on a schedule. I cannot tell how much she's getting. I don't know how long she should nurse. This whole thing feels like a shot in the dark. I'm going to do everything I can to be successful at nursing. I'll trust You to guide me.

Thank You for the gift of this time and our bonding. Thank You for the intimacy of mother and child. Thank You for the privilege of nursing. Thank You for holding back the world while we sit quietly. I'm so proud of us both. You have given us a special time of love and closeness. You are an amazing Creator.

AMEN.

For you will nurse and be satisfied at her comforting breasts; you will drink deeply and delight in her overflowing abundance.

—Isaiah 66:11

SIMPLE PLEASURES

DEAR LORD,

Happy day! Being unpregnant brings many pleasures. Things are relinquished and almost forgotten.

Thank You for relief from indigestion and a stuffy nose that cleared up with delivery. Thank You for the real joy of sleeping three hours without needing to visit the bathroom. Thank You for the ability to bend over and get out of a chair unassisted.

I can even run and jump if I wish. I can hug my children without someone else in between. I can see my feet when I look down, and I can tie my shoes all by myself. I don't have to worry about drinking too much water before I get in the car. I haven't even bumped my tummy against anything for days now. I didn't appreciate all these little things until they were gone, but I certainly appreciate them now.

Thank You that a belt is in my future and that baggy jeans might work pretty soon. Thank You for the regular clothes that already fit and for maternity clothes that are now too big. Thank You that I can sleep close to my husband, with his arms reaching all the way around me. Thank You for the renewed option of sleeping on my stomach. Thank You for the quietness inside.

God, You are very good to me. I breathe a Thank-You prayer each time I remember that You are restoring all that my body sacrificed for pregnancy. Because You are a God of life and a God of restoration, You are more than worthy of praise. From my grateful heart, I praise You for simple pleasures.

AMEN.

How great is your goodness, which you have stored up for those who fear you, which you bestow in the sight of men on those who take refuge in you.

—Psalm 31:19

A SHOWER FOR BABY

LORD,

What a sweet blessing! All the ladies from church joined together and provided a shower for Anna Grace this afternoon. On a Sunday, the weekend before Christmas and right before the cantata, they managed to squeeze in two hours of quiet celebration. In a festive home with fantastic food, the gift of a shower was very special.

So many came and held our sleeping treasure. They brought us every variation of pink and honored us with heartfelt words of admiration. Perhaps my greatest gift was the opportunity to introduce our two-week-old bundle of joy to my friends. At times, pride can be righteous and good. Today, I felt "bursting-at-the-seams" proud.

Thank You for the best part of the day. Grayson knew we were going to a baby shower. It never occurred to me that he had no idea what that meant. When we got there he ate a snack, took off his shoes, and ran to play with friends. At the end of the party, I called out, "Grayson, it's time to go." And bless his pure, four-year-old heart, he came running and began taking off his clothes. "Hang on," I said, "we're getting ready to go." With the most innocent look on his face, he answered, "But Mama, we can't go. I haven't had my shower yet." I struggled to maintain my composure. Thank You for this story I'll enjoy telling his children, Lord.

And bless all the gift givers, preparers, and friends. Return to them the blessing they have given. In Jesus' name,

AMEN.

On coming to the house, they saw the child with his mother Mary, and they bowed down and worshiped him. Then they opened their treasures and presented him with gifts of gold and of incense and of myrrh.

—Matthew 2:11

33

ON MY OWN

GOD OF MY STRENGTH,

When Mama left last night, it felt like my whole world left with her. I barely endured the ride to the airport. The good-bye at the gate proved one of the most difficult of my life. I wanted to hold onto her and scream, "Please don't go!" or throw a tantrum. Anything to keep her from going. It seems like my parents always leave when its time for me to grow again.

The day I entered college, they drove me down, helped me unload my belongings, took me to lunch, then left. I can still remember the shock of watching them drive away, leaving me with 40,000 strangers. When it was time for graduate school, they drove me halfway across the country, then left again. Later when I got married, I couldn't believe they let me pack all my things into a moving truck and drive away with this guy. Each time, I wanted to hold on, but they wisely let go, forcing me to stand on my own.

Lord, help me regain my composure. Help me to find confidence in my strengths. May my eyes behold the beauty of this time. Although it feels like the earth is giving way, I have longed for this journey. The truth is, You are within me. You help me, and I will not fall. I am not "on my own," for the Most High God dwells in the holy place of my soul. The knowledge of Your love and the assurance of Your presence truly make me glad. In Your strong name I pray,

AMEN.

God is our refuge and strength, an ever-present help in trouble. Therefore we will not fear, though the earth give way and the mountains fall into the heart of the sea, though its waters roar and foam and the mountains quake with their surging. There is a river whose streams make glad the city of God, the holy place where the Most High dwells. God is within her, she will not fall; God will help her at break of day.

—Psalm 46:1-5

SLEEP–DEPRIVED

FATHER,

I feel tired—more tired than I have ever felt. I stumble through the days and nights. Still elated, yet very exhausted, this rundown, worn-out mommy is taking sleep deprivation to a whole new level.

I amaze myself with my adeptness for staggering through the house at night, feeding the baby; changing diapers, clothes, sheets, and blankets; calming little cries; and getting up in thirty minutes to do it all over again. Thank You for the inspired person who scheduled a Martha Stewart broadcast at 3:00 A.M. Now I can learn how to fold napkins or build a compost heap during our early morning feedings.

I now understand why new mommies don't brush their teeth, take showers, change clothes, or put in their contact lenses. They can't. Eight pounds of pure innocence now rule their lives. Baby's needs dominate and when the baby sleeps, why waste time on hygiene? It's time for Mom to sleep, too.

Lord, I smile at my exhaustion. It's so worth it. I'd take it double if I had to. But it does make me incredibly grumpy. I'm okay as long as I don't need to make a decision, get ready to go anywhere, prepare a meal, or carry on a conversation. Ask me to function as my old self, and I'm pushed right over the edge, the ragged edge of mothering.

I am so dependent on You right now. You are my companion. You are my strength. Teach this Heaven-sent angel to close her little peepers and rest—rest long and rest much. I trust that slumber will come soon. From my groggy heart, I pray.

AMEN.

He grants sleep to those he loves.

—Psalm 127:2

PEACE

LORD,

There is too much craziness in my house. I'm not ready for all this chaos to resume. People run in and out. Our schedules fill again. My "things to do" list grows. I have this sense that my family and friends expect that I'm back to normal. I'm not. We're not. In case nobody noticed, I just had a baby!

I still yearn for the quiet and uncomplicated. No expectations. No agenda. No rules. Just me and my baby, falling in love with each other, spending the days in leisure. These days are so precious. I want them to last. I want to savor their taste. I'm not ready for soccer practice, church socials, PTA meetings, or car-pooling. Yet I'm being thrown back into the world. I feel my precious days slipping away.

Lord, I invite You to come. Stand right in the middle of my family and give us Your peace. I need a little more time to regain my composure. I want to sit still and just hold my baby. I need to sleep for a long, long time. Pour out Your grace on all of us. Slow down my hurried family.

I'm so glad that the world's expectations are not Yours. You don't esteem busyness and crowded lives. You honor tender hearts and quiet moments. I look to You for guidance—a slow and steady re-entry. My children need their mama. My husband needs his wife. I am willing but still weak.

I pray in the powerful name of Jesus, Who gives peace.

AMEN.

Jesus came and stood among them and said,
"Peace be with you!"

—John 20:19

NOTHING ACCOMPLISHED

DEAR GOD OF SOLOMON,

Our disheveled bed remains unmade another day. It's lunchtime and I still haven't eaten breakfast. I've attempted to unload the dishwasher for hours now; just a few more free moments and it will be done. Diapers and blankets and spit-on clothes clutter every catch-all place. The garbage can is full . . . well, maybe I can cram in a little more trash. It's Thursday, and Sunday's paper waits to be read.

A new baby. How can one precious, cherub-faced newborn bring such devastation and disarray? I thought I was ready for the challenge, but here I sprawl, knocked flat. My greatest daily accomplishment is survival. My kids go through each day semi-clothed and partially fed. We quickly gave up on the goal of getting anywhere on time. We are just about ready to leave, and there's another poopey diaper or spit-up. Spit-up is the worst. Most of the time I have to change my clothes as well as hers, then clean up the car seat and any other object within projectile distance.

My preoccupation with accomplishment is freed by the words of Solomon, "What has been done will be done again" (Ecclesiastes 1:9). Some things take lower priority. "Catching up" only lasts for a moment. These are the days of mothering my baby. Caring for my family is important. My attitude is important. Loving You is important. Everything else can wait. Nothing else really matters right now.

Thank You for the release from accomplishment. Help me to focus on the things that matter. There is rest in the truth of Your Word.

AMEN.

"Meaningless! Meaningless!" says the Teacher, "Utterly meaningless! Everything is meaningless." What does man gain from all his labor at which he toils under the sun? . . . All things are wearisome, more than one can say. . . . What has been will be again, what has been done will be done again; there is nothing new under the sun.

—Ecclesiastes 1:2–3, 8–9

A GOOD MAN

DEAR GOD,

Marriage—what a shot in the dark! You see a person on his or her best behavior for roughly a year. You fall in love. You pray and pray. You make an uninformed decision based on everything you think you have in common. You factor out sin, childhood traumas, and different cultures. Then, you go for it.

I remember hoping against hope that Paul was as good as he seemed. Thank You, God, he is better.

Thank You for every part of our marriage. Thank You for the really hard days that force us to grow up. Thank You for the tender moments that hold us together. Thank You for choosing a great complement for me. He can say, "No," when I would always say, "Yes." He can think of fourteen different options, when I struggle to come up with one. He is right-brained. I barely have a brain. We both love people. We both love our family. We make a great team.

The birth of this child brought a time of great intimacy for us. Loving someone else deepens our love for each other. My husband, like me, finds joy in just watching our baby sleep. We both laugh when she wrinkles her nose. He shares my joy over her slightest accomplishment. It is so good to know him as a friend.

Lord, continue to strengthen our love. Inspire great passion. Let us grow in maturity and wisdom. It will bless our children if we love each other deeply. Teach me how to love my husband well. I will learn from You.

AMEN.

Husbands, love your wives, just as Christ loved the church and gave himself up for her.

—Ephesians 5:25

THE MELTDOWN

MY SAVIOR AND GOD,

I'm experiencing a complete emotional meltdown. I suppose it was bound to happen. Fatigue to the tenth power combined with too many commitments, too many telephone calls, too many icky diapers, and too many lonely days. Today, I came undone. Uncontrollable sobbing. Toddler-like babbling. Enough was enough. My body couldn't take anymore.

Thank You for a husband who didn't know what to do, but still did the right thing. He sent me to bed. An exhausted, irrational woman only needs one thing—sleep. Thank You that he took the baby and the children and just rode around until he had to come home. Thank You that he never asked, "What's wrong with you?" Thank You that he's pretending that my teary-eyed fit never happened. I don't need the extra guilt.

Lord, I put my hope in You. I ask You to restore my soul. Help me to pace my days. Keep me from being overtaken by the urgency of everyone else's needs. Give me resilience in the face of monotony. Increase my portion of strength. Lengthen my time of rest.

I cry out to You from my brokenness—a heap of shattered pieces, I desperately need to be put back together by You. Secure my world. Grant the strength that only You can give. Please provide me the power to face each new challenge. Bestow upon me enough wisdom to know when to stop . . . to know when I have done all I can do. I pray through the tears. I trust You to provide. I love You forever and pray in Your name.

AMEN.

Why are you downcast, O my soul? Why so
disturbed within me? Put your hope in
God, for I will yet praise him,
my Savior and my God.

—Psalm 42:11

45

MY WEIGHT—UGH!

MY GOD WHO UNDERSTANDS,

Here I sit, wearing really tight shorts and an oversized shirt, eating a fat-free cracker, sipping my fifth glass of water, and praying about my weight—again. These are hard prayers. They make me sad. I know that I just had a baby. I know that my body will take a while to recover. Okay, I know I shouldn't compare. However, when I see thin women holding young babies, my extra 40 pounds feel like 200.

Lord, I do want the prize that comes from self-control and discipline. I want health and fitness. I want to be around for a long time to watch my little pumpkin grow up. I want to function in this world without guilt and embarrassment. I am wasting too much time lamenting. I'm ready to be free. I'm ready for a victory. I'm ready to do whatever it takes.

I ask that You keep my heart and mind focused. I must stay motivated and committed to the race ahead of me. I see the prize. I don't want to forfeit any more years to my battle with weight. I don't want to be a slave to my body. There are many more great things that I can do with all that energy and emotion.

I must rely on the power that comes from You. I am weak and wobbly. I need Your strength. I will keep praying, over and over, as I run toward the prize—running to win. Only by Your mercy will I find victory. I look forward to giving You the glory. Thank You in advance.

AMEN.

Do you not know that those who run in a race all run, but only one receives the prize? Run in such a way that you may win. Everyone who competes in the games exercises self-control in all things. . . . Therefore I run in such a way, as not without aim; I box in such a way, as not beating the air; but I discipline my body and make it my slave.

—1 Corinthians 9:24–27 NAS

47

New Hope

OH, FAITHFUL GOD,

Anna Grace slept for five hours last night. I feel like a new woman! Thank You. Five hours of sleep gave me so much more energy today. I feel rehabilitated. I actually feel like doing something. I might cook a real meal tonight. Maybe I'll even make a dent in the laundry.

With a rested body, I'm re-energized and ready to go. My attitude is better. My heart is hopeful. I am encouraged by the gift of Your compassion—a sign that this season of exhaustion and seclusion really will soon pass.

Being a mother is my greatest joy. Yet there have been days of excruciating loneliness. I want to be here. I want to be full-time and on-call. Still at times I feel left out and isolated, like a hermit-mom with barely a peek at the "real world." I allow the clouds to creep in and thicken. I tend to forget that seasons pass quickly. I forget that You always remember. You see my long days. You care for me in my loneliness. You are ever-present.

Thank You for Your faithfulness. Thank You that a bit of sleep could open my eyes. I had lost myself in the fatigue and, in the process, lost sight of my hope. Now my faith has been renewed, along with my body. You breathe fresh life into my spirit. Today, I am a better mother for my children and a better wife for my husband. I am so grateful for Your tender mercies.

Bless You God. You knew exactly what I needed, and You provided. You have blessed me today.

AMEN.

Yet this I call to mind and therefore I have hope: Because of the LORD's great love we are not consumed, for his compassions never fail. They are new every morning; great is your faithfulness.

—Lamentations 3:21–23

PURE LOVE

GOD OF LOVE,

The ability to fully embrace the verses of
1 Corinthians 13—the Love Chapter—has always
seemed to elude me. To purely apply it to my life
seemed impossible, beyond my capacity . . . until
now. For me, to love my baby and my children is
to begin to know pure love. Only through them
am I coming to understand the depth of Your love
for me.

I have come to possess a patience I never
thought possible. Its origin must certainly be this
well of pure love that has been filled by the birth
of my babies. I never knew the depth of comfort I
could give until one of my own was sick. I never

thought I could truly love someone else more than myself. But when love is pure, it comes so easily.

To have a child, and then remember that You love me as Your child, gives me new insight. Now I know why You say that You will never stop loving me. How could any good mother stop loving her child? I see why You intervene to discipline and protect. What decent parent wouldn't do the same? I feel more secure about Your promises for my future. Just like a child, I trust in Your provision, my providing Parent.

I commit my unending love to my babies. With Your help and through Your fathomless love, I will do my best to always protect, always trust, always hope, and always persevere. May my love for them never fail. May I extend to them the pure and eternal love that only You can give.

AMEN.

Love is patient, love is kind. It does not envy, it does not boast, it is not proud. It is not rude, it is not self-seeking, it is not easily angered, it keeps no record of wrongs. Love does not delight in evil but rejoices with the truth. It always protects, always trusts, always hopes, always perseveres. Love never fails.

—1 Corinthians 13:4–8

SHARED JOY

FATHER GOD,

A wonderful part of our "Anna Grace blessing" is found in sharing this abundant joy with friends and relatives. What fun I had designing a birth announcement, introducing her to the world, and proclaiming our delight and gratitude. With each address, I imagined our friends joining us in the celebration of her birth. When they realized she was number four, most of them probably celebrated the fact that she is ours—not theirs! Either way, the birth of our child creates a great reason for rejoicing.

The abundance of cards and gifts brings sweet blessings as each one expresses heartfelt acknowledgment of shared joy. And the joy continues every time someone peeks into her car seat or asks if they can hold the baby. I am very proud. With great delight, I share her.

Do You, too, share in all this excitement? I know that You do! I imagine that You smile like a proud father at every birth. It must thrill You to introduce each of Your new and precious creations . . . to watch parents experience the most phenomenal event on earth . . . to witness the unbelievable power of love. Surely, the birth of each baby is Your personalized proclamation of extravagant love and commitment to us all.

Lord, thank You for the joy You have given us to share. She is amazing. You are so generous to entrust her to us. We will continue to share her with others and remind them that she is a gift from Your gracious hand. From my heart of joy, I find it a pleasure to pray.

AMEN.

When it was time for Elizabeth to have her baby, she gave birth to a son. Her neighbors and relatives heard that the Lord had shown her great mercy, and they shared her joy.

—Luke 1:57

FREE TO SAY "NO"

LORD,

I expect too much of myself. I pretend a full recovery. I tell myself that I feel good. I push myself to get back into a routine. I do all the laundry and attempt to prepare balanced meals. I run errands and pick up dry cleaning. I meet a friend for lunch and make polite conversation, silently wishing I had stayed home in bed. I feel like I am stretching the limits of sanity. I had a baby only three weeks ago.

I should simplify and free myself from these self-imposed expectations. These ought to be the days that I live in the bounty of Your grace. This should be a time for supper that comes to the door or through a take-out window . . . wrinkled clothes . . . a clear calendar . . . no voice mail, no e-mail, no pagers, and no cell phones. Above all else, I must learn how to remain guilt-free when my mouth wrestles out the word, "No."

Lord, I know these pressures are mine, not Yours. I live as though there is someone keeping score. I am miserable and failing. I sense that You prefer for me to be still and rest during this season. I desperately desire this also. There is no game to win. No one is keeping score. There are no trophies for worn-out moms.

Thank You for the comfort of Your love and Your complete acceptance. Thank You for the lessons learned when I say, "No." Because of Your leading and by Your strength, I will live in the freedom that You offer. In Jesus' name,

AMEN.

Simply let your "Yes" be "Yes," and your
"No," "No."

—Matthew 5:37

HEAVEN EYES

MY DEAR GOD IN HEAVEN,

What a delight and a mystery to watch Anna Grace. Seemingly too young to respond, in her sleep she can smile the grandest smiles and even laugh aloud. She will stare at the ceiling as if intently watching something. I wonder what she sees? I wonder what causes her laughter? I wonder if she still sees through "Heaven eyes"? Can she still glimpse the angels who came with her from Heaven? Do they make her laugh out loud? Do they sing her to sleep? Do they make her smile while she dreams?

I know that You assign angels to watch over her. For this I am very grateful. Thank You for supernatural supervision. I find comfort in knowing that heavenly defenders protect my precious treasure. You appoint guardian angels and give them direct access to You. How much You must care for little children.

I cannot envision an angel, but I believe. I cannot comprehend Your greatness, but I believe. I cannot understand the mysteries of Heaven, but I believe. I believe that You love me. I believe that You are the Master Creator and a compassionate God.

I would love to have "Heaven eyes" in order to behold Your supernatural work. But by faith, until that day when I have new eyes, I will believe that there is so much more than I can see.

Thank You for all that You do, both seen and unseen, to care for me and my family. Thank You for angels that come and protect babies and make them smile. By faith, I pray by all the power that is in Heaven.

AMEN.

See that you do not look down on one of these little ones. For I tell you that their angels in heaven always see the face of my Father in heaven.

—Matthew 18:10

LONGING FOR PRAYER

LORD,

Praying doesn't come easy these days. I remember the times when I could be alone with my Bible, praying until my heart overflowed. Those were sweet times of worship. But things have changed. I miss being consistent. I feel hungry for time with You.

Life's schedule has gone awry. My quiet time turns into sleepy time. My prayer life crumbles. I go to church, but my brain stays home. Thank goodness for my verse-a-day calendar or I might never read Scripture. I feel like a spiritual wipeout. I've seen it happen before—another mother bites the dust. Discouragement overwhelms me.

Please know that I love You desperately. I long for my study time. I desire to pray again. I want to be close to You. I willingly accept all these new demands in my life. I joyfully devote myself to constant interruption. Yet . . . my heart finds it difficult to make the transition. How can I be a godly woman, growing in Christ, while still performing the duties of a devoted mother? Both require time. The balance evades me.

God, I must trust You to meet my spiritual needs. I believe that You understand these days of mothering and that Your grace covers all my inconsistencies. I have a peace about this time of my life, but I desire more of You. Maybe my soul simply longs for Heaven. Perhaps my desires will only increase until I am with You. *Oh, for more of You and less of me,* my yearning heart prays.

AMEN.

Devote yourselves to prayer, keeping alert in it with an attitude of thanksgiving.

—Colossians 4:2 NAS

DISCOURAGED

MY DEAR FRIEND JESUS,

Since the day of Anna Grace's birth, our emotions have soared and hovered among the mountaintops. Somehow the whole world seemed better. People acted nicer. Our future appeared brighter. As our newly-revised family bonded together, we felt stronger. We began to dream bigger dreams. But the old world came up to meet us today, and I mourn our reacquaintance.

Discouraged. Deflated. Dry. Disillusioned. My spirit wilts. My heart grieves. There are no tears, just pure sadness over the attitudes of others. What seemed to be, is not. Our dreams took a blow. We have lost our strength. I pray for Your peace. Grant tender restoration to our torn hearts.

With our thoughts and minds so focused on the sweet and pure innocence of our baby, we almost forgot that we still live in this world. We forgot that trusts can be broken and expectations can be dashed. We forgot that some folks will do anything to achieve power. We forgot that this side of Heaven, life can sometimes be very, very hard.

Lord, I know that fullness will not transpire and tribulations will not cease until I meet You face to face. And so, I need the courage that only You can offer. Courage to press on when I would rather retreat. Courage to trust again. Courage to speak bravely, despite opposition. I stake all that I am and the future I hope for on the promise that You have overcome the world. Because the One Who overcomes has also saved my soul, I now thankfully pray in Your name.

AMEN.

These things I have spoken to you, so that in Me you may have peace. In the world you have tribulation, but take courage; I have overcome the world.

—John 16:33 NAS

COME LOOK AT HER

DEAR GOD OF GREAT JOY,

Even at 2:00 A.M., I don't really mind the cries and feeding. I truly delight in just one more look. I cannot get enough. I love to stand and stare at her. I love to see her sleep. I adore her yawn. I watch as her eyes follow the mobile, and I am happy. I work around the house for a few minutes, then give in to the urge to go peek at her again. With every glimpse of her perfect face, I breathe a prayer of thanksgiving. My soul rejoices over her.

Her half-smile and inquisitive stare entrance me. I call everyone to come and look at her when she is wide awake and curious. Thankfully, our whole family loves to marvel at this gift who breathes and sleeps and eats. I want my heart to memorize each one of these moments, things not captured by video or camera—her touch, her smell, the emotion that consumes me when I look at her.

Oh God, I continue to rejoice in the birth of our daughter. My days may be long and extremely tiring, but just one more look can revive my joy. I feel so grateful to You for the wonder of her. I never imagined the breathtaking beauty of motherhood. What a fabulous view! The most spectacular place on earth must surely be our nursery, with the priceless treasure sleeping there.

Thank You so much for the privilege of parenting. Thank You for each tender look that warms my heart. My greatest blessing is motherhood. I love You. I praise Your great name.
AMEN.

May your father and mother be glad; may she who gave you birth rejoice!

—Proverbs 23:25

FIRST CHRISTMAS

DEAR GOD IN THE HIGHEST,

It is our baby's first Christmas. It's Your Baby's birthday. What a blessed celebration. Christmas seems more intimate for our family this year. Every light seems brighter. Every ornament looks beautiful. Every carol resounds within my heart. New meaning comes to old traditions. With a new life in our family, great joy fills this season.

A baby in our home brings renewed significance to Christmas. I look at our baby and think of You. She reminds us to remember the simplicity. I consider Your sacrifice and complete humility. The God of the universe, our Lord God Almighty, poured Himself into the form of a baby. The Son of God willingly left His Father and the glory of Heaven to become a wholly dependent newborn infant. A little Baby wrapped in cloths and lying in a manger. Soft cries. A hungry child. A doting mother. God really became man. There was majesty in the manger. There were lullabies from Heaven.

How can this world, full of people, celebrate Your birth with such brilliance and fanfare, yet live their lives in disbelief? Do they not see that this singular event changed the whole course of humanity? Do they not know that myths eventually die and legends are forgotten? Yet the truth of Your birth remains.

Lord, give us eyes to see. Long before there were sugar cookies, strings of lights, and gifts under the tree, a Baby lay in a manger. His name was Jesus, and He came to save the world. Glory to God in the highest and on earth, peace for all men.

AMEN.

But the angel said to them, "Do not be afraid. I bring you good news of great joy that will be for all the people. Today in the town of David a Savior has been born to you; he is Christ the Lord. This will be a sign to you: You will find a baby wrapped in cloths and lying in a manger." Suddenly a great company of the heavenly host appeared with the angel, praising God and saying, "Glory to God in the highest, and on earth peace to men on whom his favor rests."

—Luke 2:10–14

OUR PEDIATRICIAN

ALMIGHTY PHYSICIAN,

As always, You proved Yourself faithful. We felt so sad to leave behind our wonderful doctors when we moved from Nashville to Florida. Then you graciously led us to Dr. Kimberly Bougoulias. What a blessing to know her as our pediatrician and to love her as a sister in Christ.

I count it a privilege to pray for her. I pray that her vast wisdom and insight increase. Although she is already well-trained and extremely conscientious, I ask that You continually keep her fresh and alert. Settle her heart and renew her mind daily. Go with her into each exam room. May she be prepared to correctly diagnose and recommend accurate treatment.

Give her enough time to be thorough with each young patient. Rekindle her passion for healing. Increase her patience for screaming babies, cranky kids, and worn-out mamas.

She means so much more to our family than a doctor for our sicknesses. She provides a wealth of knowledge when I'm unsure. When I am anxious, she calms and encourages. She speaks with a strong voice in the middle of my night. I listen intently to everything she says. I trust in the integrity of her advice and insights.

Lord, use her as a vessel of Your healing and protection in our family. Thank You for a woman who depends on You and believes in You as the Great Physician. Bless her family and her practice. Return to her many-fold the goodness and kindness she gives. Thank You for the peace You provide through our pediatrician. Thank You for protecting us through the discipline of medicine. Thank You for the one who cares for our health. In Jesus' name,

AMEN.

If any of you lacks wisdom, he should ask God,
who gives generously to all without finding
fault, and it will be given to him. But when
he asks, he must believe and not doubt, because
he who doubts is like a wave of the sea,
blown and tossed by the wind.

—James 1:5–6

FIRST SMILE

JESUS,

My world stood joyously still today. I peeked in on the baby and she smiled at me. No, it wasn't just gas. There was no mistaking it. This was no fluke or a quirky little smile. She looked thrilled to see me. Her whole face brightened. Her arms waved and her feet got happy. Her eyes sparkled. She tried to make gurgling noises. She did everything her little body could do to tell me that she loves me.

Wow! I cannot formulate words to completely describe the condition of my heart. Abundantly full. Content. Wildly happy. Moved. Her smile exhilarates. She inspires me to be a great mama. I am bursting with every motherly emotion. Compassion. Tenderness. Protection. Devotion.

There is truth in Your words. A mother does forget her pain as she comes to know the great joy of her child. I would gladly do every miserable day all over again. Love is such a mighty thing. Love captivates and surprises me. I never dreamed that I had the capacity to love so purely.

Lord, thank You for the smile that has made me stronger. My resolve increases. I want to learn how to love my daughter well. I commit to treat her delicate little spirit with great respect. These are the tender years when character develops; let me gently care for the heart and mind on the other side of her smile.

Does it move You when we look up and see You and rejoice in Your presence? Oh, Lord, I hope You are pleased by my love and deep admiration for You. I pray that my life will show You that I love You.

AMEN.

A woman giving birth to a child has pain because her time has come; but when her baby is born she forgets the anguish because of her joy that a child is born into the world.

—John 16:21

Our Circle of Friends

LORD OF MY HEART,

Thank You for our circle of friends. They stood with us through pregnancy and delivery. They helped us pray this baby safely here. They mourn our loss of sleep with us. They rejoice with us in each new accomplishment. They hold us up. They make the hard days bearable and the good days brighter. We are better parents and better people because we have great friends.

Meals, cards, telephone calls, gifts, and flowers—our friends give so much of themselves. Yet the blessings just keep coming. With our extended family far away, our friends have stepped in and loved us with a "family love." Our neighbor sends us "extra" soup and cookies and produce from the farmer's market. Two sweet women come and sit with the baby while I go in the next room and write. One family came over to keep our children, then extravagantly paid for our date-night. We cherish these gifts of time and treasure.

Lord, let me always possess a grateful heart. Help me to recall how awesome it feels to have supper delivered—free. I don't want to forget how wonderful it is to be ordered out of the house with my husband for the night. Let me give to others with the abundance I receive. I am inspired to love lavishly because of the generous love of my friends.

I know that each friend is a gift of Your grace. You hug us through their arms. You love us through their lives. Thank You for loving our family through an incredible circle of friends. In the power of Your love, I pray.

AMEN.

A friend loves at all times.

—Proverbs 17:17

THE FOURTH BABY

MY LORD AND MY FATHER,

Four babies in seven years. Wow! I look in our mini-van's rearview mirror and cannot believe they are all ours—one happy little youth group. Every outing turns into a major expedition. Car seat, booster seat, infant carrier, double stroller, two diaper bags, snacks for the crew, extra bottles for the baby, and everyone's favorite toy, just for a trip to the mall.

With the arrival of Anna Grace, kids now outnumber parents two-to-one. This means eighty nails to clip. Eight socks to find. Eight shoes to tie. Sixteen daily diaper changes. Four mouths to feed. And well over a million tears to dry. Comedy, drama, and live entertainment pack each day. Curtain calls and encore presentations fill our nights. I expect that at least one of my children will be up every night for the next twenty years. Perhaps I'll sleep sometime later in the millennium.

Lord, thank You. Although I feel like a crazy person most of the time, I am also incredibly happy. Joy fills our home. The fun times are much more fun and the bad times not nearly so tragic with a house full of giggling, wiggling children. Each one is a treasure. Each one a reward. Each one a blessing.

Thank You for four. Thank You for giving us more children than we as parents could possibly handle on our own. That means we must trust You more. We have to believe in You for provision. May our faith increase. Thanks to Your way of doing math, one plus one has made four. May each one of us bring You honor. In Your precious name,

AMEN.

> Behold, children are a gift of the LORD; the fruit of the womb is a reward. Like arrows in the hand of a warrior, so are the children of one's youth. How blessed is the man whose quiver is full of them; they will not be ashamed, when they speak with their enemies in the gate.
>
> —Psalm 127:3–5 NAS

She'll Call Me Mommy

DEAR FATHER, MY GUIDE,

I walk into the room and my daughter jumps with great excitement. Her eyes dance and her feet kick. She watches my every move with tremendous delight. I look into her bright blue eyes and realize that I am the one she'll be watching for a very long time. I am the one who will teach her how to act like a lady. I am the one who will model godliness and grace.

When I call her name she turns her head to remind me that I am the one she will listen to. She will learn about caring and attitude and love from the inflection of my tones and from the choice of my words. She will laugh a little like me and cry about the things that make me cry. Then one day she'll say to herself, I cannot believe it, I sound just like my mother.

In my mind, I imagine the person I want her to see when she watches me. That person is a God-fearing woman, tender and strong. A woman who laughs easily. A woman who loves endlessly. A woman I am still striving to be. I know that my child watches me, Lord. She makes me want to be that woman even more.

The responsibility is great, and the years are few. I fall on Your mercy and ask for divine intervention and assistance. For the sake of my children, let me be a mother whom they can call "blessed." Because little eyes see and little ears hear, I commit to continue praying and growing. In Jesus, I am able.

AMEN.

Her children arise and call her blessed.

—Proverbs 31:28

When a Baby Cries

LORD OF MY STRENGTH,

She's come undone. I've come unglued. I don't know what else to do. Our sweet little baby is crying and crying. I checked her diaper. I tried feeding her. Nothing appears to be wrong, but I can't seem to do anything right. Laying her down brings screams. Rocking brings no comfort. The only thing that gives us a respite from the wailing is walking. So we walk all through the house, dancing and swaying and humming in the dark.

I'm tired, Lord. I wish I could crawl up in someone's lap and cry, but I am the mother. I am the holder and protector. I am the giver of love and affection. I'm supposed to be strong, but I find myself depleted.

Lord, You know that I need an incredible amount of patience. The doctor says that the baby is adjusting to this world in the only way she knows—crying. She needs the security of being held, comforted, and soothed. She needs me to be patient and strong. She needs tenderness and compassion. All these qualities would come much easier if the clock didn't read 3:00 A.M.

God, You are my only source of strength and help. Only You can turn her weeping into shouts of joy. I ask You to come quickly and rescue us. Give calm and assurance to her little spirit. Let her rest peacefully. Give me strong arms to hold her for as many nights as she cries. Let me run to her with compassion and shower her with the love of a mother. Because You are strong when I am weak, I pray in Your name.

AMEN.

Weeping may last for the night, but a shout of joy comes in the morning.

—Psalm 30:5 NAS

Praise be to the LORD, for he has heard my cry for mercy. The LORD is my strength and my shield; my heart trusts in him, and I am helped. My heart leaps for joy and I will give thanks to him in song.

—Psalm 28:6–7

A Day Away

PRECIOUS FATHER,

Thank You for a day away with my friend. Twenty-four precious hours to fly a few states away, watch a show, stay up late, giggle a lot, and re-board a plane headed for home. My body feels absolutely worn out, but my spirit soars.

I am a better mom because of this time. I interacted with adults all day and into the night. I feel full, almost talked out. I read the paper on the plane and worked on some writing projects I had carried along. I ate my whole bag of pretzels without sharing. I enjoyed great conversations with straight lines of reasoning. What a pleasure to remember what it is like to talk to someone without distraction! I was able to look into their eyes and actually hear what they were saying.

I am surprised by how much I can accomplish when there are no diapers to change or mouths to feed. I read and prayed without interruption. I took in so much and gave very little. I felt like I had forgotten something the whole time I was gone. I didn't realize that I spend most of my day cuddling and soothing and holding.

Yet what a blessing to be Mommy. I may get away for refueling, but my spirit yearns to return. I missed all these little people who need me. I longed for hugs and slobbery kisses. I craved the joy that truly does come from giving.

Life is back to normal now, just as if I'd never left. However, I hold in my heart the pleasure of going and the delight of returning. Thank You for the gift of a day away. In Jesus' name,

AMEN.

For they refreshed my spirit.

—1 Corinthians 16:18

DaDaDa

ABBA DADDY,

Between Anna Grace's laughter and cries, her first syllables were finally uttered—DaDaDa. Barely discernible at first, it is now her very best trick. She has yet to attach any meaning to her new language, but it won't be long until Paul walks into the room, and she will scream with delight, "DaDa!"

I pray with great fervency that she will always know the joy of Daddy. If I have learned one compelling truth thus far, it is that a child's character is framed by their relationship with their father. God, I pray that Anna Grace will know the deep, deep love of her father.

I pray for the two of them. May they enjoy many tender days together. Little tea parties in her room. Late night snuggles and prayers. Tickling. Giggling. Lots of "date-nights." Books read out loud. The father/daughter dance. The singing of silly songs. Special trips to the store. Surprises in his pockets.

Please grant Paul an abundance of wisdom and a deep well of patience. Teach him how to love each of his children well. Give him the ability to seek out each of their differences and encourage them in their giftedness. For the rest of their lives they will be impacted by their daddy's words . . . "I love you . . . Great job . . . I am so proud to be your father." Let him be extravagant with his adoration. He lays the strong foundation upon which they will build the rest of their lives.

May Anna Grace, William, Grayson, and Taylor come to know You as Abba Daddy because their earthly daddy has provided a great introduction. Only by Your leading,

AMEN.

Listen . . . to a father's instruction; pay
attention and gain understanding.

—Proverbs 4:1

EXHAUSTED

DEAR JESUS,

We attended the church picnic yesterday. It was a covered dish, "bring enough for your family plus one" occasion. I began cooking the night before, preparing a huge lunch, making everything from scratch. In the afternoon, we hauled all the kids, baby gear, food, chairs, and toys over to the park. I felt tired, but it was going to be worth it for the great food and fellowship.

My first disappointment came when I realized that only a few people had actually cooked. Almost everyone else stopped by the deli for chicken, potato salad, and bags of cookies. What was I thinking? Why do I always do too much? Try too hard? Make things more complicated than they have to be? Why was I determined to have fresh salad and cake from scratch when everyone else seemed satisfied to gnaw on a cold, store-bought chicken leg?

Then while I held Anna Grace and balanced a Styrofoam plate on my knee, I overheard two men talking behind me. "Yeah, you can tell she has a new baby because she looks tired all the time."

Crushed, my spirit sank. Their words were true. I do look tired all the time. I am tired all the time. I am exhausted . . . spent . . . completely drained.

A part of my weariness is this season of life. The other part of my weariness comes from poor choices. Gourmet picnics can come later. This is a time for quick meals from a drive-through window. I come to You because I am at the end of myself. I need Your rest. I need Your wisdom. I need You. I love You.

AMEN.

Come to me, all you who are weary and burdened, and I will give you rest. Take my yoke upon you and learn from me, for I am gentle and humble in heart, and you will find rest for your souls. For my yoke is easy and my burden is light.

—Matthew 11:28–30

IN A BLINK

OH, LORD,

She grows so fast! It seems like we just brought Anna Grace home from the hospital yesterday. Now she is rolling all over the floor. She holds her head up high to survey the world. She can reach for anything and eventually find a way to get it in her mouth. She's just about to outgrow the infant carrier. We skipped right past nine month-sized clothing. Where have the days gone?

When I was a child, time seemed to drag by so slowly. I remember thinking the fourth grade was the longest year of my life. It felt like I wore a size 6X forever. Birthdays took a whole lifetime to come again. Christmas arrived even slower. The days seemed longer, because there was only me to think about and few responsibilities.

Now the days sail by. There is so much to do. The little sweetie who used to sleep all the time now needs only one-and-a-half naps a day. The baby who once sat and leisurely watched the world go by now wants—no, demands—some interaction. I feel like I turned around twice and my newborn became an infant.

In a blink, she'll be grown. It rips my heart out to think about it. Lord, if there's any way that I can hold these days in my mind, please let it happen. Let me linger at her bedside. Let me hug a little longer. Let me sing one more song. Let me rock long past her falling asleep. By Your mercy, I will remember all of these days and give You praise.

AMEN.

And the child grew and became strong; he was filled with wisdom, and the grace of God was upon him.

—Luke 2:40

A HARD MARRIAGE WEEK

LORD,

It was bound to happen sometime. Add a baby to the household and everybody must figure out how to adjust. Although I know why it happened, the effect proved paralyzing. Paul and I have endured a very hard marriage week.

I thought we had been talking to each other, but then one day we just weren't. One silent day turned into several. Before we knew what had happened, we were angry. Not just the "I'm hurt" kind of angry, but the "I'm going to say something ugly" kind of angry. Accusations and unfortunate words finally broke the deafening silence—untrue words—certainly not the kind of words you say to the most important person in your life.

We've been here before, but I thought we'd grown past it. Instead, we wallowed around in our frustrations for a couple of days, and then something unprecedented happened. We talked on a level we've never gone to before. We usually just "get over" these things and do our best to pretend they never happened. But this time, I believe that You intervened to pull back some layers and connect us at a deeper level.

God, in the past, I prayed that You would strengthen our marriage. I asked You to prepare us for the challenges ahead. And I believe that You used the relationship fire of this past week to make us stronger. I still feel a little winded from the whole ordeal, but I do believe that I know my husband better now. I reaffirm my commitment to love him well. I declare that I am powerless on my own, but able by Your grace. In Jesus' name,
AMEN.

Let us not become weary in doing good, for at the proper time we will reap a harvest if we do not give up. Therefore, as we have opportunity, let us do good to all people, especially to those who belong to the family of believers.

—Galatians 6:9–10

NAP TIME

LORD,

All is quiet on the home front now. Thank You for nap time! I call this my "Daily Sanity Hour." It's a sacred time to refuel and reflect and attempt to remember what I was trying to do five hours ago, before everyone woke up. When the baby finally gives in to her exhaustion and closes her eyes, it feels like a gift. I gently close her door and appreciate these precious moments You provide. This "all to myself" time refreshes my spirit. I know it makes me a better mommy.

During nap time I try not to do anything that I can do with the baby in her swing. I don't even talk on the phone unless it's with a kindred friend. I give out little pieces of me all day long, so I have to fight for this time alone. At some point, I just have to stop and let You refill my empty places. My soul doesn't get replenished when I mop the floor during my quiet time. And You know what it's like when I try to operate out of emptiness. It's not very pretty.

Father, during today's nap time, please lead me beside quiet waters. Restore my soul. Fill me with the glory of Your presence. Encourage me with Your Word. I lay all my efforts before You and ask for Your priorities and perspective. Set my mind on eternal things. Let me hear from You. Teach me to listen. May I give to my family from the overflowing cup that You provide. I bless You, my Shepherd and my Savior.

AMEN.

The LORD is my shepherd, I shall not be in want. He makes me lie down in green pastures, he leads me beside quiet waters, he restores my soul. He guides me in paths of righteousness for his name's sake.

—Psalm 23: 1–3

LAUGHTER AND DANCING

SWEET JESUS,

Surely we are born for laughter and dancing. Our baby proves it to me. Her laugh is among the finest and purest I have ever known. She cackles aloud at the most surprising things. A "Hello" from one of her brothers can send her into a wave of silliness and giggles. Simply the delight of her own laughter produces jitterbug feet and cha-cha arms.

Thank You that she laughs so effortlessly. May it always be so. Protect her heart and her spirit from the things that might rob her joy. She is completely innocent and pure. I know that the world will come around to find her one day, but may she always remember how to laugh from her heart.

I once heard a man say that he could tell a lot about people by the way they laugh. I have come to believe the great truth of his words. Real laughter—spontaneous, readily available, and unmanufactured—can only come from a person of peace and contentment. It only comes from a person who is looking for joy.

Let her always look for joy. Let her know the good medicine of rib-splitting laughter and impromptu dancing. May she learn this fine art from her parents. Fill our home with comedy and wit, ballet and The Flat Rock Stomp, great fun and silliness. You gave us marvelous gifts when You gave us a time to laugh and a time to dance. Thank You for life's fun. Thank you for a baby who reminds us all to loosen up a little, look for the joy, and giggle. From our immense pleasure, we give You praise.

AMEN.

There is a time for everything, and a season for
every activity under heaven . . . a time to weep
and a time to laugh, a time to mourn
and a time to dance.

—Ecclesiastes 3:1,4

91

MY NEIGHBOR'S EMPTY ARMS

FATHER,

I know many women still wait for children, but I cry today especially for my neighbor and friend, Amy. Every month of their eleven-year marriage, she has longed and hoped for a child. Her heart breaks because her arms remain empty.

It couldn't have been easy to have three kids and a newborn move in next door. Yet she loves You deeply. Her spirit is radiant despite all the questions. Questions like, *Why can my twin sister have children and I cannot? Why do all my friends get pregnant without trying? How could anyone abort a baby whom I would desperately love to mother?* She is one of the strongest women I know. Even with a wounded heart and in the midst of her longings, she stands up and takes on the world everyday. You must surely be the One Who gives her courage. You must be the One Who provides her with strength.

Lord, I say aloud, "I don't understand either." Amy and her husband are wonderful. They are Christ-like. They are great givers of love. They would be outstanding parents. Why? Why can't they have a child? I echo their prayers and ask boldly that You would give them their heart's desire.

Until then, please give them great comfort. Teach our family how to love their family. I believe that we have come to live beside them for a purpose. Remind me of days that might be especially hard for Amy. Give me wisdom on how to encourage her. I commit to be a prayer warrior on her behalf. Please answer these prayers for Amy.*
AMEN.

*The Lord did answer this prayer. After eleven years of trying, Amy is now nine weeks pregnant and loving every day of being sick.

Hannah had none [no children]. In bitterness of soul Hannah wept much and prayed to the LORD. And she made a vow, saying, "O LORD Almighty, if you will only look upon your servant's misery and remember me, and not forget your servant but give her a son, then I will give him to the LORD for all the days of his life."

—1 Samuel 1:2,10–11

He settles the barren woman in her home as a happy mother of children. Praise the LORD.

—Psalm 113:9

ROAD TRIP

FATHER,

Finally, everyone—and everything—is packed into the car. Thank You! To arrive at this point required a long week of preparation. I somehow forgot that a new baby multiplies luggage requirements by ten. The five older members of this family needed one bag each, but the baby nearly required her own U-Haul. Diapers, wipes, baby food, formula, stroller, toys, and a portable crib are crammed into every corner of our van. I still don't know if we have everything, but at this point I don't care.

Two hard days of travel lie ahead of us, and already the baby has screamed for an hour. Finding herself strapped into a car seat for an excursion that takes longer than a grocery store trek definitely does not excite her. God, I pray for her little spirit—and for ours. Give her the ability to soothe herself. Grant me patience with her frustration.

While we travel, Lord, I pray for safety. Keep us alert and wise. Protect us from the unseen dangers all around. Assign angels to guard our precious cargo. Carry us safely to our destination. Give rest to our bodies in the hotels where we stay. Shelter us from the weariness that might rob us of all the joy from our vacation.

I trust You to go before us and prepare our path. Make this trip lots of fun. Thank You for the extended family that waits on the other side of these miles to meet and welcome our newest member. What a joy it will be to introduce her to all the people I love! Thank You for the adventure of her first trip. I sure do love You!

AMEN.

The LORD watches over you — the LORD is your shade at your right hand; the sun will not harm you by day, nor the moon by night. The LORD will keep you from all harm—he will watch over your life; the LORD will watch over your coming and going both now and forevermore.

—Psalm 121:5–8

HER MOTHER IS YOUR CHILD

MY FATHER,

Some mornings I wake up thinking, *How can I possibly be the mother? I still feel so much like a child.*

Most of me grew up, but a part of me remains young and insecure and afraid. For brief moments, I want to be little again. I want to go to my room and play until supper. I want someone else to make all the decisions. I want to be quiet and shy and carefree.

But I am the mother. I am a tower of strength. I am a governing authority. I am a schedule maker. I am a travel taker. I am a provider and lover and instructor. I am a leader. How did I get here so fast? Wasn't the prom just yesterday? But now . . . now, I am the woman of many hats, the mother of a new baby, the wife of a busy man.

Lord, is there a reason I wrestle with these feelings? Will the little child inside keep me forever dependent on You? Will You always let me crawl up in Your lap, lay my head on Your chest, and be comforted by my Daddy? Then maybe it's good. Maybe it's good to let the little girl in me need the Daddy in You.

In those moments when I feel like the child, Lord, remind me not to fear. I am not alone. I have not been abandoned. I am held tightly by my awesome Father. I am led by my Abba Daddy. What a blessing for my baby that her mother is Your child.

AMEN.

And he said: "I tell you the truth, unless you change and become like little children, you will never enter the kingdom of heaven. Therefore, whoever humbles himself like this child is the greatest in the kingdom of heaven."

—Matthew 18:3–4

IT'S LONELY OUT HERE

GOD OF MY STRENGTH,

Perhaps the most misguided question anyone could ever ask a new mother is, "So, what have you been doing all day?" Sometimes, I feel like saying, "Actually, I don't know what I've been doing. I've just been redoing the things I've already done. I re-fed the kids I already fed. I re-washed the clothes I already washed. And I re-diapered the child I already diapered. I've been in this house all day by myself, being the best mommy I can figure out how to be. I fought to survive and managed to hold onto my attitude. That's what I've been doing all day."

Lord, the truth about what I've been doing is that I've mostly been feeling lonely. It's lonely here in "baby land." Of course there are the children and the endless list of chores to do. We play and laugh and do fun things, but I still long for grown-up conversation. No wonder so many women love Oprah. By late afternoon, it's a blessing to listen to an intelligent woman speak to you for an hour.

Perhaps I'm afraid that all this monotony and repetition will deplete my inner passions. I'm afraid that I'll forget how to talk and interact with some adults. I'm afraid that life will spit me out on the other side of kids, and I'll be a lost old woman, wondering what happened to the world.

Father, I have to trust that You see my needs and hear my cries. I must believe that, in these very lonely times, You will be my portion and strength. When I am lonely, I will cling to the truth of Your presence.

AMEN.

Whom have I in heaven but you? And earth has nothing I desire besides you. My flesh and my heart may fail, but God is the strength of my heart and my portion forever.

—Psalm 73:25–26

THE WEDDING

MY LORD AND MY GOD,

We escorted all the children, baby included, to my brother's wedding yesterday. What a fabulous celebration of love and commitment. The bride looked amazing, and my brother was full of adoration for his new wife. Thank You for the strength of their faith and their love for one another. I ask that You pour out Your blessings on their marriage in the years ahead. May they grow in godliness and love.

As I sat proudly in our family pew, the realization hit me. In just a few years, I will be the woman in the motherly dress standing to watch as my daughter walks down the aisle. I will be the teary-eyed mess winking to my son as he takes his place center-church. One day it will be our babies, all grown up and ready to leave. One day some ugly boy will steal the heart of one of our angels. One day a giggly little girl who can't boil an egg will cleave to one of our sons. One day soon, it will be our turn.

Lord, I need to release all of this to You right now. When it's time (in about forty years), please give our children the ability to choose for love and to choose for keeps. Help me to love each new family-member-by-marriage with a mother's compassionate love.

Thankfully, the first great life adventure looming on the horizon is still just kindergarten. Yet praying for their weddings reminds me to hug them long. Because I know You have a great plan for each one of their lives, I can rejoice in all the years to come. By faith, I pray.

AMEN.

For this reason a man will leave his father and mother and be united to his wife, and they will become one flesh.

—Genesis 2:24

MY BABY-IN-LOVE

SWEET GOD,

What a privilege it is to pray for our babies' future mates. Imagine! There may be four children somewhere out there in this big world who will one day become our "babies-in-love." Our children will choose them to love and to cherish forever. And we will welcome them into our home and love them as our own.

Wherever they are, Lord, I pray that they will know great devotion and protection. Let their parents love them with a mighty love and shelter their hearts from evil. I pray for a childhood that is tender and carefree with lots of play and laughter. Let somebody tell them over and over how much they are loved and adored. Give them the security of a family and a place to call home.

Inspire their learning and increase their bounty of common sense. Let them come to know You as Savior at the earliest possible age. Give them wisdom in their life choices. Encourage them to choose purity and wait for the true love of our child. Show them the blessings of walking with You.

My heart is glad to pray for the other babies who will grow up and come to our family through love. Remind me to pray for them often. You know them by name, and I smile to think that, someday, our babies will meet the ones You have in mind for them.

Because I believe in the power of prayer, and because I want the best possible mates for our children, I will pray until I meet our "babies-in-love." May Your will be done. Because I love You, I will trust You.

AMEN.

Do not be yoked together with unbelievers. For what do righteousness and wickedness have in common? Or what fellowship can light have with darkness?

—2 Corinthians 6:14

A wife of noble character who can find? She is worth far more than rubies.

—Proverbs 31:10

Husbands, love your wives, just as Christ loved the church and gave himself up for her to make her holy.

—Ephesians 5:25–26

FROM WHOM ALL BLESSINGS FLOW

MY GOD FROM WHOM ALL BLESSINGS FLOW,

I thank You for:

The absolutely astounding miracle of birth.

A healthy baby.

Grandparents and doting friends.

Lullabies and a rocking chair.

The ability to nourish and hush little cries.

One proud Daddy.

Three equally proud siblings.

A place that we call home.

Big blue eyes that stare back at me.

More than enough love for everyone.

Great laughter.

Contentment.

The overwhelming sense of Your presence.

Hopes and dreams for the years to come.

You shower us with one blessing after another. You are so good to always do more than we can imagine. I love You and bless You.

AMEN.

From the fullness of his grace we have all received one blessing after another.

—John 1:16

OUR SICK BABY

OH, GREAT PHYSICIAN,

Today, our tiny angel wrestles with her first fever and infection. After a very long night, we are both worn out. It broke my heart to listen to her cry out in pain when I laid her down. She could only get comfortable enough to take little naps in my arms. So, we rocked and walked all night. Morning couldn't dawn soon enough. We had to be the first in line at our pediatrician's office.

When we arrived, I quickly realized we weren't the only distressed parents in town. The line formed quickly with all the other moms and dads holding their teary-eyed, pajama-clad children. Obviously, they had also been up all night, taking temperatures and measuring ibuprofen. We were all comparing symptoms and lamenting our little one's sickness.

Lord, thank You for the nurses and our kind pediatrician. What a welcome relief to trust my suffering daughter to these qualified professionals for diagnosis and care. Thank You for their compassion and tenderness. Thank You that the doctor noticed the concern in my eyes and spoke to my fears. Thank You for an antibiotic that will restore health.

I pray for complete healing for Anna Grace. Nothing else seems to matter when our baby is sick. Please restore full health to her body. Remove all the infection, and give her an afternoon of good rest. Give me wisdom as I provide comfort and help. Lord, I thank You in advance for the healing You will bring. By the power of Jesus, Who healed those who were in need, I pray.

AMEN.

But the crowds were aware of this and followed Him; and welcoming them, He began speaking to them about the kingdom of God and curing those who had need of healing.

—Luke 9:11 NAS

And the prayer offered in faith will make the sick person well.

—James 5:15

SIBLINGS

LORD,

How thrilling to think that this baby will grow up with a sister and two brothers! Surely, siblings are among the greatest gifts we can give our children. Long after Mom and Dad are gone, the bond of brother/sisterhood remains. During these important early years, they build the foundation of their sibling relationships. Certainly, it will be easier for them to climb courageously into the world with a safety rope tied securely to family.

We look to You for all wisdom and guidance. Train us in the art of nurturing their sibling friendships. Keep us from fueling their rivalries. Teach us how to take four unique individuals, applaud their differences, strengthen their passions, and knit them together as a family.

We have already taught the older ones to say, "I promise to take care of you forever. I will always love you. Friends forever." The out-loud "God, bwess Anna Dace" prayers of her two-year-old brother shower Anna Grace. We make them hug each other long, say, "I'm sorry," and ask one another for forgiveness.

As parents, we attempt to model loyalty and trust, but our efforts will be fruitless without You. Only You can provide the faithfulness that binds siblings together. You alone put into their hearts a love that cannot be broken. If they can become friends, they will be each other's greatest source of support and encouragement. However, it is only through Your supernatural power that they are able to be marvelous life-long friends. May they always live together in such unity. In Jesus' name,

AMEN.

How good and pleasant it is when brothers live together in unity! . . . For there the LORD bestows his blessing, even life forevermore.

—Psalm 133:1, 3

A BATH TIME PRAYER

DEAR LORD,

Bath time brings such beautiful moments with my baby. She loves the warmth of the water. Splashing is already her favorite game. A bath always pacifies and relaxes her fussy, ready-to-go-to-bed body. This nighttime ritual helps wash away the day and prepare her for a sound sleep.

As I bathe her, I pray for her body. I pray that she will continue to grow in strength and in stature. Give her strong legs to run and play and do ballet. Arms that can knock a ball right out of the park. A heart that will last for a long life. Vision and hearing and the ability to speak. Strengthen her mind so she can learn and process and develop. Protect her from injury and disease.

So much goes on under that skin. I must trust that nothing goes unseen by Your watchful eye.

What a privilege to hold in my arms a place where You abide. What a privilege to hold onto a temple. Lord, I pray that, in addition to caring for her physical body, You would care for her tender little spirit as well. Protect her soul until she can choose You for her own. Shelter her mind from any harm. Guard the precious wellspring of her heart.

I commit to do all that I can to care for this one. I entrust all that I cannot do to You. When I hold my fresh-smelling baby in a big fuzzy towel, I am moved by the greatness of Your gift to me. Thank You for her. I love You.

AMEN.

Don't you know that you yourselves are God's temple and that God's Spirit lives in you?

—1 Corinthians 3:16

BABY STUFF

LORD,

First-time parents feel certain that they need all the latest "stuff" before a new baby can enter their home. But it doesn't take much parenting experience to realize less is so much better! They grow so fast and use much less than we originally expected. Still, "new and shiny" is incredibly tempting. The balance concerning baby stuff easily escalates into a battle.

Over the years, I've learned one thing about "stuff." If you buy all that great baby gear, someone has to take care of it and carry it. With our first baby, I carted along half the nursery on every outing. I definitely had the over-prepared, uptight mommy look perfected. I packed the diaper bag and prepared for every conceivable emergency, then ended up dragging it around.

By baby number four, we have learned to travel light. Our diaper bag now holds only a cloth diaper, a bottle, regular diapers, and wipes. My attitude is a little lighter, too. A dribble no longer demands a change of everyone's clothes. My self-worth isn't destroyed by a few stains. And I no longer yearn for the newest things in the baby store. I've learned that their usefulness is so fleeting. A few clean, old things work just fine.

Thank You for taking away my hunger for new baby stuff. Thank You for teaching me that what I put into my child matters more than what I put on my child. Why does it often take years to learn simple truth? My child is my treasure. To look anywhere else is a distraction to my heart. Thank You for another lesson in the eternal. From Jesus' teaching, I grow and I change.

AMEN.

Don't hoard treasure down here where it gets eaten by moths and corroded by rust—or worse—stolen by burglars. Stockpile treasure in heaven, where it's safe from moth, rust, and burglars. It's obvious, isn't it? The place where your treasure is, is the place you will most want to be, and end up being.

—Matthew 6:19–21 THE MESSAGE

EVERYTHING TO GOD IN PRAYER

LORD,

In my pre-baby days, I found lots of time to stop and pray. Now I walk and pray . . . cook and pray . . . rock and pray. With this new baby, I find a renewed passion for prayer, yet my time for concentrated prayer and meditation is practically non-existent. I offer to You my prayer life and ask You to deepen my walk and strengthen my life.

I know that there is no power in my life without prayer. Without prayer, the hurdles that pop up in the day seem insurmountable. I find myself spinning in the same circle without progress. My mind replays the same defeating thoughts over and over. My spirit lacks enthusiasm. My ambition stumbles. My mind wanders.

You understand how easy it is to forget to pray. Mothering is totally consuming. There is always another task waiting for completion. There is always someone who needs attention. There is always something or someone distracting my prayers. I laugh to remember the many times I have knelt in my room, only to have someone crawling on my back a few minutes later. I keep praying and they keep playing. Eventually, they work themselves up under my face and whisper, "Mommy, whatya doin'? Me pray too."

But, Lord, I commit to keep trying. I need what You give to me in prayer—vision, fresh perspective, encouragement, comfort, forgiveness. A new baby brings even more reasons to pray in all things, without ceasing. I am thirstier now than ever. I must continue to run to Your well and drink deeply. The water is sweet and lifegiving. Because I have tasted Your goodness, I will pray. I love You.

AMEN.

Do not be anxious about anything, but in everything, by prayer and petition, with thanksgiving, present your requests to God. And the peace of God, which transcends all understanding, will guard your hearts and your minds in Christ Jesus.

—Philippians 4:6–7

A PALE SHADE OF GREEN

FATHER,

I come to You with a confession. Sometimes it's difficult to look around and see what other people have without wrestling envy. I know that You bless us with everything we need—make that, more than we need. But when I see a Suburban, I want one! I envision hauling lots of kids along with a week's worth of groceries without anyone stepping on the bread. In truth, my mini-van does fine as long as I keep the bread on my lap.

When I go into a house with a bonus room, I feel myself pushing past admiring and into coveting. A designated toy room with a door you can shut . . . just the thought of it makes me sigh. Housekeepers turn me a little green, too. How frivolous and dreamy to imagine someone else wiping the toothpaste off the front of my cabinets.

But Sundays are the days I feel the greenest; for my husband works in a church, and there are times I wish that he didn't. It's nothing big, really, just that little pang I feel when I struggle through the Sunday morning routine alone. Then when I pull into the church parking lot with all my kids, I look over to see some dad walking in with his family.

Lord, I lay all this before You. I know this feeling takes up space in my mind. I don't need to waste any more thought-time on things that don't really matter. Take every ache of envy and turn it into rejoicing. Remove the desire for things I don't need. Forgive me for being so petty. You have blessed me. I know it.

AMEN.

Since we live by the Spirit, let us keep in step with the Spirit. Let us not become conceited, provoking and envying each other.

—Galatians 5:25–26

IT'S TIME TO CRY

DEAR GOD,

Our pediatrician told us at the two-month check-up, "It's time to let Anna Grace learn how to cry herself to sleep."

"Already?" I asked, "She still seems so little."

Then came the doctor's words of wisdom, "Angela, mothering is about knowing when it is time to let go. This is the first occasion for you to learn how to let go." Yuck. She just got here. I don't want to let go.

I knew she was right, but I procrastinated for a few months. Finally, I decided the time had come to give it a try. I waited until Paul was out of town. I knew he hated hearing Anna Grace cry even more than I. The first night she cried for twenty minutes. I sat on my bed with the baby monitor and cried too. The second night she cried for five minutes. The third night she calmed herself and went right to sleep. It worked. She has gone to sleep by herself ever since. I guess the doctor knew best.

Thank You for this great lesson. Thank You for teaching me again that structure and discipline are good for a child, even when it's temporarily unpleasant or difficult. Thank You for the affirmation that my role as a parent includes leading and setting boundaries.

I desire a harvest of righteousness and peace in our children. I want the goodness that comes from training. From Your leading and through wise counsel, we seek to do what is right. From You, we will learn how to "train a child in the way he should go" (Proverbs 22:6). In Jesus' strong name, AMEN.

No discipline seems pleasant at the time, but painful. Later on, however, it produces a harvest of righteousness and peace for those who have been trained by it.

—Hebrews 12:11

Train a child in the way he should go, and when he is old he will not turn from it.

—Proverbs 22:6

LOW ESTEEM

LORD,

I could pretend. I could act bold and courageous and strong, but You know that I'm not. The vivacious person I used to be now works very hard to blend into the woodwork. I feel myself consciously trying not to call attention to myself. My eyes drop a little lower. I stand back a little more. I leave a little sooner. I'm so proud to be a new mother, but I keep hoping they see her—not me.

I look in the mirror and wonder, *Who is this woman with the pimply face and old lady hair?* I think about the extra forty pounds I'm lugging around, and I feel profoundly sad and ashamed. I make unfair comparisons—the kind that always leave me coming up short. I don't want to be fat and dowdy and plain. I know the me I used to be still lives in here somewhere. I don't like this new version of me.

Lord, I look to You to revive my esteem. Guilt and embarrassment are quite paralyzing. It has taken hold of me far too long. I refuse to sacrifice any more days to my insecurities. Renew the steadfast spirit that You have placed within me. Give me the confidence I need to overcome my lack of discipline.

And for these days, may I have grace—the precious grace that You give to sinners and whiners and people who want to do better? I know that You love me, and I commit to press on toward the goals I have in mind. By Your power, I am able.

AMEN.

Create in me a pure heart, O God, and renew a steadfast spirit within me. Do not cast me from your presence or take your Holy Spirit from me. Restore to me the joy of your salvation and grant me a willing spirit, to sustain me.

—Psalm 51:10–12

121

A PURE LIFE

BLESSED JESUS,

A friend of mine recently returned from a personal retreat. From his time of prayer and solitude, he determined that more than anything, he desires to live a pure life. My heart also resounded with his proclamation. I, too, want to live a pure life. I want to teach my daughter to live purely. But what does it mean for a new mother to practice purity?

To live a pure life means I cannot be swayed from my purpose to glorify You—in my home and in my choices—no matter what happens. Whatever the world throws at me, no matter how persuasive or alluring it might be, I will hold on for dear life to the biblical principles that Jesus calls me to exemplify.

Pure mothering means that I won't always be popular. I'll probably always be different. It means that I'll learn to forgive when the world begs me to remember. It means that my path will sometimes be narrow. It means that I'll finish what I start. It means that I'm not afraid to dream big dreams or set high standards.

The pure heart of a mother looks into the eyes of her child, and says, "I will never, ever give up on you. I will love you and pursue you. I will train you in what is right. I will require of you what is good." And by Your mercy, dear Jesus, make me pure. Let me pass on a pure life of love. Let me be a woman who will see God. For Your glory, I strive.

AMEN.

Who may ascend the hill of the LORD? Who may stand in his holy place? He who has clean hands and a pure heart, who does not lift up his soul to an idol or swear by what is false. He will receive blessing from the LORD and vindication from God his Savior. Such is the generation of those who seek him, who seek your face, O God of Jacob.

—Psalm 24:3–6

Blessed are the pure in heart, for they will see God.

—Matthew 5:8

123

MOTHER'S DAY

MY LORD,

A Mother's Day baby dedication sounded like a great idea when we planned it—sentimental and spiritual. Then as always, reality hit. Just as soon as I get the notion that I can live a whimsical greeting-card-type life, the world blasts in to remind me, "Life is hard. Days are long. Sometimes it is a fight just to keep standing!"

I promised to meet Paul at church just before the service. That meant getting up even earlier than usual. Bathing four children. Feeding three children. Nursing a baby. My shower. My hair. My makeup. Diaper bags. Corsage. Hair bows. A beautiful hand-made gown. Whew! Boy, were we running late.

I broke into an unladylike sweat while loading the mini-van, then zoomed off toward the church. I hadn't gotten very far before I was quickly detected by local radar.

"Can I see your license and registration?" the officer routinely questioned as he looked at all my smiling kids. They were just thrilled to meet a real live police officer. "Where were you going Mrs. Guffey?" "You say you've lived here eight months. Did you know that you only have thirty days to obtain a Florida license?" "Did you know that you were doing sixty-one in a thirty-five?" I just wanted him to hurry up and hand me the ticket. I would have cried, but I didn't want to ruin my fresh make-up.

"Mrs. Guffey, I want you to get a Florida license. I want you to slow down. And I want you to have a happy Mother's Day." No ticket. No fine. Lots of grace. Lord, thank You for the great, great lesson that comes from not getting what I deserve.

AMEN.

And God is able to make all grace
abound to you.

—2 Corinthians 9:8

Our Baby's Dedication

PRECIOUS LORD,

It felt as if someone was missing—like we were still waiting for someone who belonged to us. So Paul and I prayed and asked if it might be Your will for us to parent another child. Our family was busy, but we seemed incomplete somehow. You were so gracious to answer, "Yes." Another child was indeed a part of Your plan for our family.

Now we come to dedicate the life of Anna Grace Nicole to You. We know, full well, that she is Your treasure. You only lend her to us for a while. We promise to take care of her and love her with all our might. We promise to teach her that You love her even more than we do. We promise to give parenting every valiant effort.

Lord, we come to this task completely dependent on You. Give us great wisdom and discernment in the decisions ahead. Temper our discipline and instruction with gentleness and grace. Help us to always consider how our actions and words may affect the Spirit of God inside her.

There is no way to predict what the years hold for our family, so we must walk each day in total surrender to Your plan and Your purpose. We take every step assuming that You have already supplied the courage and resources we'll need. We dream and hope for the future, expecting that You're already there.

We thankfully dedicate our child to her Almighty God and Creator. Work in her life to Your glory. Keep her set apart and protected. From the depth of our gratitude, we praise You.

AMEN.

I prayed for this child, and the LORD has granted me what I asked of him. So now I give him to the LORD. For his whole life he will be given over to the LORD.

—1 Samuel 1:27–28

Yet you brought me out of the womb; you made me trust in you even at my mother's breast. From birth I was cast upon you; from my mother's womb you have been my God.

—Psalm 22:9–10

127

A MOTHER'S LOVE

MY HEAVENLY FATHER,

I didn't know I possessed the ability to love like a mother until I had children. Again, with this baby, I reaffirm my love and commitment. In Your presence, I promise to:

Keep her clean and clothed and fed.

Do whatever it takes to model goodness and godliness.

Care greatly about her character.

Discipline her.

Tell her about Jesus, her Savior.

Love her daddy.

Rejoice with her on the good days and hold her on the bad ones.

Be interruptible for the rest of my life.

Read to her and sing to her and teach her to dance.

Introduce her to the rest of Your creation.

Praise her.

Be a well of deep grace she can always come home to.

Give her strong wings and a desire to fly.

Mothering is a high and holy privilege. More than anything else, I want to finish well. I solemnly dedicate my entire lifetime to this great purpose. May You be pleased with my offering. By the power of Christ Jesus,

AMEN.

The woman whose son was alive was filled with compassion for her son and said to the king, "Please, my lord, give her the living baby! Don't kill him!" But the other said, "Neither I nor you shall have him. Cut him in two!" Then the king gave his ruling: "Give the living baby to the first woman. Do not kill him; she is his mother."

—1 Kings 3:26–27

129

SOLID FOOD

FATHER,

We have new instructions from our pediatrician, "It's time for solid food. Continue with her cereal, but add vegetables, meat, fruit, and table food as she's interested." No one knew that she was interested until she tasted her first spoonful of pureed carrots. Yum, yum. She got so excited that she tried to gurgle and blew carrots all over us both. What fun to watch her delight in taste. What fun to watch her try new things.

Her growth happens so fast! Every week there is a new accomplishment and another stage of development. Seemingly overnight, her body has matured and become hungry for more. Her little personality is maturing too. She already has distinct likes and dislikes, as evidenced when she happily pops her mouth open for bananas or makes a sour face after trying broccoli.

In this part of her life I have someone to guide me; someone to say, "Now, she is ready. Stop what you were doing and begin something new." There are guidelines to follow concerning development and readiness. But what happens when she grows off the charts? What happens when we must decide on our own when she's prepared for the next life step?

I pray that You put discernment inside me to know when she's ready for more. I assume that You have innately equipped me to "just know" when my children need to take the next step. I depend on Your guidance and pray for understanding. By trial and error, by prayer and counsel, we will know when our child is ready for more. I'm leaning on You. I love You.

AMEN.

Anyone who lives on milk, being still an infant, is not acquainted with the teaching about righteousness. But solid food is for the mature, who by constant use have trained themselves to distinguish good from evil.

—Hebrews 5:13–14

FIVE NIGHTS OF SLEEP

FATHER,

Oh, thank You for five full nights of great sleep. The baby seems to have found her routine. Now we're sleeping for at least eight hours at a stretch. She's even begun to play in her crib after she wakes up—long enough for me to get dressed and get her cereal ready. I offer You my most sincere praise and appreciation. What a blessing to sleep in peace!

I am grateful for the quiet rest. It makes a difference in my attitude. I no longer spend the whole day looking for a nap. I am no longer completely frustrated when all the children won't take a nap at the same time. About 3:00 this afternoon, I expected to give out as usual, but the consistent sleep gave me new energy. I've spent a long time as a sleep-deprived mommy. Thank You for rescuing my weary body.

As long as we have children at home, someone will probably be up in the middle of the night for something. Many nights, I wake up with little eyes peering into mine. I'd never say this out-loud, but I cherish those times. It's a blessing to be the one they come to—their comfort-giver, blanket-retriever, temperature-taker, snuggle-maker.

When it comes to sleep, these first baby months have been long. I wondered if she would ever learn to sleep when it's dark. Thank You for the accomplishment of slumber and the deep sigh of relief it brings. May the content of our days bring You glory. From my fresh mind and glad heart, I give You praise.

AMEN.

I will lie down and sleep in peace.

—Psalm 4:8

LAURA

DEAR JESUS,

I firmly believe that every new mother needs another new mother for a friend. Thank You for Laura, my sister-in-law, and my new-mother-friend, four times over. Thank You that we live on the same street and have had all of our babies within months of each other. We have been able to commiserate pregnancies and the price of diapers for years now.

It has been a blessing to walk together through all of our life changes. Four births. Four recoveries. Every possible new baby question. Phone time and sitting-in-the-driveway time. Laura has a great heart for giving, and we share everything imaginable. Maternity clothes, baby clothes, car seats, and quick-what-can-I-fix-for-supper recipes.

We talk about the same thing forever and never run out of patience with each other. Long after Paul tired of talking about baby names, I could drag myself down to Laura's and we'd ponder names for another hour. Who else wants to talk about nursing and baby food and diaper rash, except another new mother and friend?

When I married Paul, I had no idea that included in the package was the gift of such a wonderful sister-in-law. God, thank You for giving me Laura. Because I have spent these days with her, I am a better mother. Please pour out Your blessings on her and her five guys. Encourage her on the hard days. Give her many more mountaintops than valleys. Help her to know that You see the way she loves her family, and that You are very pleased. Thank You for the treasure of her friendship to me. You are good to me.

AMEN.

And do not forget to do good and to share
with others, for with such sacrifices
God is pleased.

—Hebrews 13:16

135

CONTENTMENT

LORD,

Everything is falling apart, but I'm okay. I know it must be You.

Last weekend, we moved from an apartment into our house. I can't find anything in our boxes except Christmas ornaments. The washing machine leaks. The compressor on the air conditioner froze up. The van needs new tires. My teething baby fusses constantly. I'm looking at unpaid hospital bills, and the insurance company cannot seem to resolve the paperwork. The mess and the stress and the heat wear us all down. But in the midst of our tattered and frayed world, You hold me together.

God, thank You for providing great contentment in the midst of great frustration. Composure and calm in the middle of mild chaos is one of the sweet rewards of pursuing godliness. I can't comprehend how the rest of the world makes it through life's guaranteed ups and downs without You.

You provide supernatural strength and assurance. You intervene with goodness and blessings. If I am committed to You, then all the areas of my life weave and work together for Your glory and for my good. I am not afraid because I know that my life is Yours. I belong to You. Everything I possess is Yours. I praise You for this gift of contentment and calm. I vividly remember the days when I would have whined and wrung my hands with worry. The peace that abides in my heart today comes from growing in grace.

When I've done everything I know to do, I'll just stand until You intervene. I trust You. By the help of Jesus,

AMEN.

But godliness with contentment is great gain.

—1 Timothy 6:6

SALVATION

JESUS,

I am privileged to pray for my daughter's salvation. My prayers for her began when she was forming in the womb. Now, I commit to continue in prayer until she believes. Luke 15:10 says that there is rejoicing in the presence of angels when one sinner repents. Heaven throws a party when one person comes to know You as Savior!

If the party is in the presence of angels, then the giver of the party must be You. When the lost are found and the old become new, You declare a celestial celebration. You initiate all the hoopla. You proclaim, "Let the rejoicing begin, my child whom I love has come home." I can just imagine dancing and singing and great anthems of praise.

If Heaven gets excited about the salvation of one, then how can I do any less? I will gladly pray for this joyous event. For each of my children, I pray that they find salvation early in their lives. Please keep them from too many wasted and wandering years. I didn't know any real purpose for my life until I knew You. May they come to know You very soon.

May Paul and I shine as beacons. Teach us to guide and not smother. May we offer Your gift without force. We want their decisions to be their own. May they soon know the tender love of Your merciful forgiveness and the joy of Your grace. May they live all of their lives sheltered by Your compassionate hand. Because You are the only way to eternal life, I pray from the power of Your sacrifice.

AMEN.

I tell you, there is rejoicing in the presence of
the angels of God over one sinner who repents.

—Luke 15:10

SEPTUPLETS

LORD,

What have I been whining about? I only have one new baby. Bobbi McCaughey has seven new babies! I think I'm just as amazed as everyone else in the world. What a thrill to learn that all seven babies had been delivered and that Mommy and children were doing fine. I prayed right along with the rest of the country that You would protect them and keep them all healthy.

I am so thankful for the strong testimony of Bobbi and Kenny. It's just like You to choose a humble family in a tiny little house to bless with seven precious babies. Thank You for this godly couple and the witness they have given to the world. They have spoken so eloquently of their love for their children and of their unwavering confidence in You. They have trusted You out loud for the whole world to hear. They have spoken with profound wisdom and clarity.

Thank You for Bobbi's great perseverance, both in mind and in body. Please strengthen her for all the years ahead. Give each one of those children healthy bodies and sound minds. I cannot imagine the task before her, but I pray with confidence in Your continued provision.

If there were a sisterhood of new mothers, I'm sure we'd all elect Bobbi president—an appropriate title for a woman who oversees a small army of little ones. To read about one day in her life inspires me to live mine a little better. Please pour out an abundance of blessings on them all. And let them shine from Your love and for Your glory. By the grace of Jesus,

AMEN.

God blessed them and said to them, "Be fruitful and increase in number."

—Genesis 1:28

IF I SHOULD DIE

LORD,

My heart desires to stay on this earth for a long time. I want to be here to love and nurture my children. I want to applaud their accomplishments and laugh at their jokes. I want to kiss all their boo-boos and take pictures before the prom. I want them to always have the arms of their mommy. I want to play hide-and-seek with my grandchildren.

But I know that my plans may not be Yours. I know that none of us know the exact hour when you will call us Home. And so, I ask You, Father . . . if I should die . . . please make certain that my babies know how deeply they were loved by their mommy. I never knew pure love on this earth until I knew them. I want them to know that they have inspired me to set higher goals. They have challenged me to love with greater passion. They have taught me how to laugh and be silly again.

More than anything, I want them to know You. If they will walk with You and listen to You, their lives will be good and anchored and noble. Teach them the value of simplicity, the pleasure of family and friends, the joy of pursuing their passions. Make sure that they learn how to laugh and live from the blessings of grace.

This must be one of the hardest prayers I've ever prayed, Lord. And don't get me wrong, I'm not planning on going anywhere. I just want You to know that I trust You. I know that You will always take care of my babies. I love You.

AMEN.

My soul finds rest in God alone; my salvation comes from him. He alone is my rock and my salvation; he is my fortress, I will never be shaken.

—Psalm 62:1–2

A MOTHER'S INTUITION

LORD,

In my pre-baby days, I feared that I possessed no mothering instincts. I never baby-sat as a teenager. Other people's babies held no attraction for me. I even remember keeping my infant nephew for a few days before the birth of our first baby. *The practice will do me good,* I thought. But oh, the joy I felt when his parents came to take him home. And I wondered if I would be an awful mother. Would I even love my baby?

Thankfully, You knew what You were doing. Intuition and mothering and adoration immediately overwhelmed me when the nurse placed my child in my arms for the first time.

Even in the hospital, I could tell when the nurse was bringing my baby, simply by her cry.

Along the way, I sometimes doubt my instincts. Instead, I listen to everyone else's advice or opinion. Yet You repeatedly reaffirm my God-given insight, instinct, and understanding.

This morning, I met a veteran-mother friend for breakfast. When the baby started to fuss, I said, "I just fed her, but I think she might still be hungry." My friend firmly instructed, "Don't give in to her. If you just fed her, she's not hungry."

I hesitated. I waited a few minutes. I tried to distract her. Finally, I did what my heart told me to do. I fed her. She ate like a champ and fell fast asleep. My friend meekly recanted, "Well, you are her mother. I guess you know what she needs."

Thank You for the gift of intuition. Thank You for whispering her needs to me. In the name of Jesus,

AMEN.

The LORD will guide you always; he will satisfy your needs in a sun-scorched land and will strengthen your frame. You will be like a well-watered garden, like a spring whose waters never fail.

—Isaiah 58:11

LONGINGS

OH, LORD,

Through the years, I have sought fulfillment in people . . . or things . . . or achievements. *Surely, at some plateau in life,* I reasoned, *all of my longings will be satisfied and my yearnings will disappear.*

But I look at life's lessons all around me, and I see people in their seventies still trying to build a bigger house and drive the right car. I see friends jumping in and out of relationships as they search for the "perfect mate." I know women who spend exorbitant amounts of money on a haircut, just so they can feel like a queen for a day.

So if marriage to a good man still leaves me longing . . . if a new baby isn't everything I need

. . . if a $400 pair of shoes doesn't do it . . . if the thrill of a Suburban won't last very long . . . if a 21-day cruise isn't enough . . . then what?

Although I stumble sometimes, I do know the answer. The longing for people and things is just my head trying to fill my heart before I reach Heaven. I will never, ever be fully satisfied until I see You face to face.

You alone satisfy my longings. You graciously sustain me and give me greater maturity. You show me the good that comes from longing for more of You. You give purpose to my want and make it righteous. You teach me what is foolishness and simply chasing after the wind.

Today, may I contentedly rest in the assurance that my joy will be complete when I enter into Your presence. Until that day,

AMEN.

For indeed in this house we groan, longing to be clothed with our dwelling from heaven.

—2 Corinthians 5:2 NAS

147

DON'T WISH HER LIFE AWAY

DEAR PATIENT LORD,

Each time I hear myself wishing her life away, I want to bite my tongue. When Anna Grace can sit up, it'll be easier to go to the store. . . . It sure will help our budget not to buy formula anymore. . . . We'll really have a lot of fun when she's walking. . . . When she's old enough for mother's day out, then I'll have a little time to myself.

Teach me to soak in this day and not wish for tomorrow. May I feel all of the hard places and remember them for a lifetime. Just for today, let me enjoy her complete dependence on me. How misguided to think that when everyone is potty-trained, when they can all dress themselves, when everyone goes to school . . . then, my life will be easy.

I yearned for this part of parenting. I wanted the tenderness and inconvenience of babies. I wanted to get up in the night, be "gacked on" more times than I can count, and change someone's diaper every two hours for ten years. I prayed for this. These are the "good ol' days." As I grow older, I'll recall them with fondness. In my heart, I don't want to wish even one of them away.

Please, Lord, remind me to savor each new day. Tell me over and over that these days are fleeting—they'll be gone in a blink. Shout to me, "The bags under your eyes and the unremitting fog of exhaustion will all truly be worth it in the end!"

Thank You for this time, Lord.

AMEN.

What is your life? You are a mist that appears for a little while and then vanishes.

—James 4:14

MONEY

LORD,

I know You provide for us. I trust You. Really. It's just that—every once in a while—I try to figure it out all by myself. I try to make the numbers work and magically multiply through the years. But by my human calculations, the math simply doesn't add up. How are we going to provide for this family? And these are the easy years with shared clothes, shared beds, and used pairs of Keds to fit any length feet. We're still living the "one-kid's-meal-and-three-plates" days.

I complain about spending $80 a month on formula. But I realize that, one day, this expense will seem like a drop in the bucket compared to the cost of basketball shoes. The other night, everyone still felt a little hungry after inhaling an extra-large pizza, and the baby isn't even eating pizza yet. I guess we'll rename "pizza night" to "pizza snack." College funds or retirement or vacations are unthinkable at this point.

We truly sensed You leading us in our decision to have four children. But now that they are all here, they need food and clothing. They need beds and drawers to hold their things. They all need to get through school somehow. Whew, I scare myself when I worry like this. Yet I know I am being totally ridiculous.

I must stand firm on the promises of Your Word. I believe that You are my Father. You know what we need. You always have and always will provide. I give You every tomorrow. By faith, I boldly walk through today. I gladly entrust our every need to You. I love You.

AMEN.

O you of little faith. So do not worry, saying, "What shall we eat?" or "What shall we drink?" or "What shall we wear?" For the pagans run after all these things, and your heavenly Father knows that you need them. But seek first his kingdom and his righteousness, and all these things will be given to you as well. Therefore do not worry about tomorrow, for tomorrow will worry about itself. Each day has enough trouble of its own.

—Matthew 6:30–34

THE RETURN

LORD,

During pregnancy, I never once longed for a dose of PMS with those dull headaches and body aches I endured for three days. The hovering grumpy cloud. An enormous craving for sleep. Feelings of frustration pulling at my insides. Not even once did I miss the emotional battle of pretending like I could handle it all.

When PMS comes to call, I want to disappear for a few days and not show my face again until it's over. I want to lock the door and hang up a sign that reads, "Mommy will be back soon. Believe me, it's in your best interest!" I wish I could fight this Pre-Monster Syndrome all alone.

But You know that I cannot go into hiding. My place is here. I long for self-control and graciousness. But over and over again, I only prove that I cannot face these days on my own. Just when I think I've got life under control, an eruption of angry emotion ambushes me. The blaze that follows in its path chars the whole family. I find myself looking through my tears at wide-eyed children who practically wonder out loud, "Who is this woman?"

Lord, this time, provide me with Your strength. Guard my wobbly emotions. Keep my mouth from saying every word that crosses my mind. Give me enough peace to neutralize the unwarranted frustrations. Lord, let me walk with You in gentleness and self-control. May a loving spirit prevail. Through Your power, I will not be defeated. By Your mercy, the monster within me will not win. In the name of Jesus I pray,

AMEN.

Come near to God, and he will come near to you.

—James 4:8

GRANDPARENTS

LORD,

Thank You for our baby's wonderful grandparents—and the added treasure of great-grandparents. Through them, we all receive a tremendous heritage of love. And oh, how they enjoy watching the family tree bloom and grow again. Thank You that our children will know them and love them and see them in action.

I pray for our little ones. May they have many years to hold onto their "mawmaws" and "pawpaws." May their most cherished childhood memories grow from the days they spend at Grandma's house and in Grandpa's yard. Give them the marvelous pleasure of being spoiled and adored—fun crafts, extra ice cream, and lazy afternoons of fishing. May the anticipation of their visits always bring squeals of delight.

Etch in their memory the times they sit on Pawpaw's lap and steer the pickup truck from the road to the house. Help them remember the sweet smell of Mawmaw's kitchen and her special muffins, baked just for them. Each December, remind them of every cold Christmas Eve that they begged to stand outside and watch Pawpaw grill steaks. Recount for them the buckets of tears they cried as we backed out of their driveway and waved goodbye.

One of the greatest gifts You have given our children is their grandparents. Bless all of the time they spend wrapped in each other's arms. Give our moms and dads long, healthy lives. May our children truly be their crown and joy. From this legacy of love, I give You praise.

AMEN.

I have been reminded of your sincere faith,
which first lived in your grandmother Lois and
in your mother Eunice and, I am persuaded,
now lives in you also.

—2 Timothy 1:5

Grandchildren are the crown of old men.

—Proverbs 17:6 NAS

SINGLE MOM

O LORD,

Two months ago, a friend with a baby the same age as mine unwillingly stepped into the ranks of single motherhood. Her husband announced that he wanted a divorce, and she was served papers that made his decree official. It seems that they had exhausted all of their efforts toward making their marriage work. Now, both are sadly alone. She struggles through each day, wounded by all the shattered, fallen pieces of her dreams. My heart grieves over her pain, and I weep for the child in-between.

Each day, I breathe a prayer for my friend. She tackles the same daily challenges I face, yet has the added burdens of double-duty parenting and a full-time career. I cannot imagine the stamina and energy her life must require. Emotionally frayed, she is forced to be courageous and strong. I don't know how she gets the laundry done or manages one minute for herself. How can she smile when her heart stands robbed and her soul abused?

God, I pray that You would quickly come to her rescue. Heal the deep hurts and bind all her wounds. Please be the Rock of her refuge and a strong fortress to save her. May she find her place in Your arms. May she know deliverance into Your righteousness. I know that You can comfort her like no other husband or lover or friend. You promise never to leave her or forsake her.

Show her the power of Your presence, Lord. Send Your Spirit to comfort her. May she be an awesome mother for her precious child. Go before her. Show her where to walk. Keep her resting in the faithful love of her Savior.

AMEN.

In you, O Lord, I have taken refuge; let me never be put to shame; deliver me in your righteousness. Turn your ear to me, come quickly to my rescue; be my rock of refuge, a strong fortress to save me. Since you are my rock and my fortress, for the sake of your name lead and guide me.

—Psalm 31:1–3

THE TABLET OF HER HEART

GOD OF ALL WISDOM,

Perhaps our greatest parenting challenge is figuring out how to write on the tablet of our daughter's heart. I mean, just how is that going to happen? Will our words be enough? Will our lives measure up to our teaching? What if we sabotage our own efforts through sin and mistakes? And how will we know that the ink with which we write is permanent ink? Won't the world try to erase all that we put in there?

I pray that I might mold the soft, pliable spirits of my children and engrave their souls with the markings of kindness and love. My prevailing ambition is to teach them about goodness and have them embrace it as their own. To show them loyalty and watch them become loyal. To give them grace and watch as they, in turn, give it to others. To introduce them to my Savior and have them choose Him for themselves.

I'm not exactly sure how this transfer will happen. I must claim the truth of Proverbs 3 for my life. I cannot lean on my own understanding. Instead, I will trust in You. In every decision I make, I will seek You. I believe that You will write on the tablets of our children's hearts, even those things that we, in our humanness, are not able to impart.

Sometimes, the enormity of our task scares me. Four precious children. Four moldable characters. Therefore, we entrust these most valuable treasures into Your hands. By Your wisdom and from Your leading, they will know righteousness all the days of their lives. In Jesus' name,

AMEN.

Let love and faithfulness never leave you; bind
them around your neck, write them on the
tablet of your heart. Then you will win favor
and a good name in the sight of God and
man. Trust in the LORD with all your heart
and lean not on your own understanding; in
all your ways acknowledge him, and he
will make your paths straight.

—Proverbs 3:3–6

TEETHING

LORD,

I see no outward signs of a tooth, but all the symptoms are there. Seven-month-old Anna Grace shows no interest in food. She acts annoyed when I try to get her to eat. Her stomach seems a little upset. Her typically agreeable disposition has turned fussy and inconsolable. She wants to munch on anything and drool on everything. Even the nipple of her bottle is useful only for chewing.

God, show me how to care for my baby. What else can I do to ease her pain and provide the comfort she needs? I know teething is a normal season in a baby's life, but she seems so incredibly frustrated. Will You provide me with the patience I need to lovingly deal with her fretting and crying?

This is just one of many times in her life when I cannot take away all of her pain. I can hold her and rock her, but she has to get through this teething process by herself. Mothers want to fix things and love all the hurts away. Mothers suffer when their babies suffer. I'm not having a good day because she's having an awful day.

Lord, give me grace for this season and every other season that follows. Let me comfort her with the comfort that You give to me. May this time pass quickly and the calm of my baby be restored. I love You for hearing my prayers and listening with genuine compassion. I love You for caring about every aspect of my baby's life. I love You for hearing this mother's prayer. Until her pain goes away, I'll pray in Your name.

AMEN.

But we were gentle among you, like a mother caring for her little children.

—1 Thessalonians 2:7

THE CALLING

LORD,

"Wake up. Stand up. Make a difference in this world!" Your call came to me many years ago, yet I remember Your words as though You spoke them yesterday. When Your call echoed in my ears, I realized that I could no longer hide behind the shelter of my family. You were talking to me—just me. You let me know in my spirit that You intended for my life to be important, to have purpose.

Before my babies, I thought that I would be pursuing my purpose and passion outside the home. I thought of my home simply as a haven for restoration and respite. My home remains a haven, but You have shown me that my calling finds fulfillment there, also. My babies are my greatest calling. Someone once said that every excellent thing in life requires much effort. Each one of my babies is incredibly excellent.

Diapering and holding, feeding and mothering, a baby remains a high and holy calling. Certainly, You ordained this season of my life. You intend it to be important and meaningful. I believe that You want me to pour out all of my gifts and cover my family with my passions. I believe that the good work You began in me does not sleep during these years; rather, it is multiplied by four.

Oh God, may I never lose sight of the calling You have placed on my life! Let me honor You and love You through my family. Because You have called, I gladly lay all that I am or ever hope to be at Your feet. In Jesus faithful name,

AMEN.

Therefore do not be ashamed of the testimony of our Lord, or of me His prisoner, but join with me in suffering for the gospel according to the power of God, who has saved us and called us with a holy calling, not according to our works, but according to His own purpose and grace which was granted us in Christ Jesus from all eternity.

—2 Timothy 1:8–9 NAS

GRACE FOR A SUPERMOM

LORD,

Today goes down in my diary as a "Supermom" day. I woke up before the birds to prepare myself and our home for dinner guests. About 6:30 A.M., all the little Guffeys tumbled out for breakfast. After quick cereal for everyone, fresh diapers, and clothes, we all climbed into the mini-van for a carpool run. I stopped at the dry cleaners, post office, and grocery store with three children in tow. Finally, we made our way home.

I spent the rest of the day attempting to make the house look like we don't have four children and trying to cook like I do it for a living. I dangled every privilege I could concoct in order to coerce the children into keeping the house clean.

I bathed them and bathed myself. I changed the baby's clothes after all three spit-up episodes. By the time Paul got home, with dinner simmering on the stove, I was just about to lose it. Tears began to flow before he could get in the door.

He found the house immaculate—and me in a mess. Of course he's witnessed this scenario before and knew just what to do. Paul shuffled everyone outside, while I went to my room to lament my "overdoing it" efforts. Why do I do this to myself? Why do I have this overwhelming urge to pretend I can do everything? I act like I can do it all . . . but You know that I can't.

Even though I'm no Supermom, You lavish Your grace on me. Thank you! In Jesus, I will be free.

AMEN.

In him we have redemption through his blood, the forgiveness of sins, in accordance with the riches of God's grace that he lavished on us with all wisdom and understanding.

—Ephesians 1:7–8

FREELY I'LL GIVE

LORD,

I stand alone in the laundry room matching 400 white socks by size and similar stains. No one sees. No one says, "Thank you." But thank You, my Lord, for this privilege.

I rock my fevered baby tenderly through the night. I change her sheets and blankets and clothes because she's sick. I do it all alone while the whole world sleeps. She'll never even remember that I cared for her. No one sees. No one says, "Thank you." But I thank You, dear Jesus, for this privilege.

I check on the little ones all through the night, re-tucking their princess sheets and action figure blankets. I say a prayer at their beds and kiss them again. They never even know that I'm there. No one sees. No one says, "Thank you." Oh, thank You, my God, for this privilege.

I mop the kitchen after everyone's in bed so it can dry before the stampede in the morning. They won't even notice that their feet no longer stick to the floor. No one sees. No one says, "Thank you." But it is truly a privilege, and I give You praise.

Truth is, the things I do all alone, in the quietness of a room or under cover of darkness, are all seen. Your steadfast eyes behold them. I have freely received from Your abundance. From such wealth, I freely give. It is a privilege to give of myself in quiet. What I once thought was sacrifice, I now count as gain.

May I always follow after Your example and give freely.

AMEN.

Freely you have received, freely give.

—Matthew 10:8

IN THE ARMS OF GOD

LORD,

When the baby startles from a loud noise, her arms flail out in search of safety. She screams instantly, voicing her fears. I run to her and hold her tightly. In my embrace, she finds comfort, protection, and soft words of assurance. Within moments, all her fears are relieved.

When she cannot see anyone and feels alone, she sticks out her lip and begins to whimper like she's lost and wants to cry. If I peek my head around the corner and say, "Hey, little sister," she'll smile. For her, everything is okay if Mommy's near.

She trusts me to feed her and always take care of her needs. She depends completely on me. In my arms, she acts like she's royalty, the queen of the world, sitting right where she belongs— propped up on the throne of Mommy's hip.

Lord, shouldn't I be the same way with You? Why do I try to fend for myself and make independent decisions, when You've called me to become like a child? I know that You want me to rest in Your arms with the assurance that You'll always care for me, always defend me, always provide, always be with me. You want me to receive from Your goodness with the heart of an infant. You want me to get back to simplicity and turn away from the complexity I've come to know. You want me to enter into Your kingdom as a child.

I want to love You as my daughter loves me. Lord, I want to love You without hesitation. Make my heart pure and child-like again. In Jesus' name,

AMEN.

I'm telling you, once and for all, that unless you return to square one and start over like children, you're not even gonna get a look at the kingdom, let alone get in. Whoever becomes simple and elemental again, like this child, will rank high in God's kingdom.

—Matthew 18:3–4 THE MESSAGE

COMPARISON

LORD,

How easily I fall into the pit of comparison! I am saddened by my lack of strong-mindedness. I see another baby and compare her outfit with the clothes my children wear. I watch another stroller roll by and remember how much it cost at the store. I walk into the home of a friend and size up the square footage in my mind. My own thoughts offend me. I know that You must be disappointed, too.

Sometimes I let the questions of others pull me into this comparison pit. "How long is your baby sleeping at night?" "Can she sit up yet?" "Do you make your own baby food?" "Are you still nursing?" "Have you enrolled her in mother's day out?" "We just got back from vacation, when is your family going?" "Do you have her on a waiting list for a private school?"

I usually handle this sort of thing without a problem. I'm okay with being different and with the individuality of our children. But every once in a while, I take an extra look. When I tally my life against someone else's, I always seem to come up short. I know better than to compare. I thought I'd matured more than this.

Father, forgive me. Please forgive my selfish pride. Change me and cleanse me, again. Point me in the right direction. Set my feet on the higher ground of love. Give me eyes to see good; blur my vision when I compare. I want to be more like You and less like me. Thank You for never growing tired of forgiving me. I love You, my Savior.

AMEN.

Each one should test his own actions. Then he can take pride in himself, without comparing himself to somebody else.

—Galatians 6:4

DATE NIGHT

GOD,

How can I thank You for such a fabulous date night with my husband? We try to get out as often as free baby-sitting will allow; and this time he planned a great evening. Our friend Lucille surprised me when she came over with supper. "Pack a bag," she said, "Paul will be home in an hour to take you away until tomorrow. I'm spending the night with your kids."

Yahoo! I was so thrilled.

Thank You for the leisurely dinner by the lake. Thank You for the cool breezes and time to talk uninterrupted. Thank You for the luxury of not needing to hurry home to relieve a worn-out sitter. How delightful to simply sit and look at the one I love. My soul is nourished. The whole night could be summed up in one word: perfect.

Our lifestyle is similar to all the other families we know. It is a struggle to keep a consistent family night, much less a regular date night. We think we're doing fine, until we finally get some time away and realize how much we've missed being alone as a couple. Thankfully, You caught us before our wells drained completely dry. You provided us with some time to replenish and refresh. We are full of renewed love for each other.

Our marriage is stronger today than it was yesterday. The sky seems a little brighter. All our problems seem a little smaller. I'm a better mommy, because of the chance to get away with my husband, my lover, my friend. Thank You for the gift of him and the gift of us together. I promise to love him forever.

AMEN.

Here is what I have seen to be good and fitting: to eat, to drink and enjoy oneself in all one's labor in which he toils under the sun during the few years of his life which God has given him; for this is his reward.

—Ecclesiastes 5:18 NAS

ADOPTION

LORD,

For years, my friend Beth and her husband waited. Then one day, the call came. The instructions were clear, "Get on a plane and fly to Romania to receive your child."

Those of us who had joined with them in prayer began to wonder if our fervent petitions would go unanswered. Then one day, You determined that the time was right. You started moving, and everything happened very fast.

Oh God, thank You for such wonderful provision. Thank You for the perseverance of two people who so desperately wanted to love a child. More than anything in this world, they longed to be parents. They willingly tackled the tasks required in order to give their love to their child.

Thank You for working through the mountains of paperwork and the years of telephone calls to unite them with the daughter You knew all along would be theirs. Thank You for their protection and safekeeping during the three long weeks in Romania.

When they walked off the plane, we rejoiced with this new mother and her child. Her pregnancy lasted much longer. Her labor pains were more intense, her yearning much deeper. But oh, the great, great joy of seeing them together. Lord, I know that You ordained them to be a family.

Please bless my dear sister, a new mother. Multiply her joy. Reward her sacrifice. Please bless the whole family. In the quietness of their home, fill them with the knowledge of Your love and faithfulness toward them. May they dance and cry and rejoice together, worshipping You for the gift You have given. I am elated for them. I am grateful to You. In the mighty name of Jesus,

AMEN.

I prayed for this child, and the LORD has granted me what I asked of him.

—1 Samuel 1:27

DADDY'S OUT OF TOWN

LORD,

On day one of Paul's out-of-town trip, I feel free. I pack him off to the airport and then we unwind. No fancy supper. No need to rush home. We play at the park and stroll around the mall until it's time to go home and get in bed. I stay late in my office after the baby goes to sleep, because no one is wondering when I'll be finished. The first day is fun. It's the rest of the days that start to hurt.

I realize by the second night that no one's coming home to relieve me. No one's coming home to talk to me. Supper seems empty. The house feels hollow. We pass the phone around so Dad can hear everybody giggle and gurgle. But it's just not the same. After we hang up the phone, we trudge off to bed all by ourselves. The children cry, "We want Daddy." I feel like crying, "I want Daddy, too." It's not so fun to stay up late the second night. I want someone to tell me to come to bed.

And now, it's a whole week without Daddy. I know he's just as empty as I am. I miss him so much. I'm thankful that, after ten years, I still want him to hurry home. Just a few more days. Lord, strengthen my heart.

We plan to make his homecoming a celebration so he will know how very much we missed him. Thank You for our good man who is faithful to work and provide. Thank You that he's coming home soon. In Jesus' name,

AMEN.

May our Lord Jesus Christ himself and God
our Father, who loved us and by his grace gave
us eternal encouragement and good hope,
encourage your hearts and strengthen you
in every good deed and word.

—2 Thessalonians 2:16–17

ROLE MODELS

DEAR LORD,

Our world cries out for good, old-fashioned role models today! Virtuous women who accept the challenge of leadership. Men who choose to be different and publicly take a stand for righteousness. People whose lives match the words they say. Where are these true-life examples my daughter can follow?

We desperately need heroes. We need spiritually healthy men and morally strong women. We need people who will humbly accept the challenge to let others emulate their lives. We need people of character, worthy of admiration. As a society, we have lost our perspective about what is good and wholesome. We let Hollywood choose our heroes and celebrities. We sit by and watch as society exalts the scandalous and reveres the obscene.

God, I pray for a better way. I pray for great heroes in our day. In these times, please give us strong people of faith. People of integrity and wise choices. Visionary individuals with talent and passion. The kind of men and women I would be pleased for my children to model and admire.

I'm not looking for someone else to raise my family. I just want to show them an alternative to what the world calls, "good." Please Lord, lift up the men and women You esteem. Grant to this generation great leaders who love You. Give them good examples to follow and outstanding teachers to imitate.

May we receive the gift of role models with humility and appreciation. May our children be blessed with godly examples of our faith. May the values they are learning be affirmed both in our home and outside our home. In the name of our Savior, our supreme example,

AMEN.

In everything set them an example by doing
what is good. In your teaching show integrity,
seriousness and soundness of speech that
cannot be condemned, so that those who
oppose you may be ashamed because they
have nothing bad to say about us.

—Titus 2:7–8

CLAUSTROPHOBIC

LORD,

My day began around 2:00 A.M. Grayson climbed into our bed for a snuggle. A few minutes later, in the dead of his sleep, he plopped his feet into my face. Enough snuggling for me! So I hauled Grayson back to his bed. William crept in a few hours later and repeated the previous scenario, but with extra wiggles. Finally, I threw back the covers and jumped out of bed just to escape from it all.

A little later, the baby woke up on the wrong side of the bed, insisting that I carry her around all day. Carrying her wouldn't have been that bad, but after breakfast, William permanently attached himself to my leg. Dragging him around with a baby in my arms wears me out.

Poor Grayson doesn't know how lucky he is just to have his shoes tied. He can hardly make his way through the crowd around Mommy. Everybody needed a mommy today. I feel claustrophobic. If one more person says, "Hold me," I think I'll cry. Mommy is pooped. I want to scream out, "Back off! Don't touch me!"

I feel like running away, but I can't. I must stay. I am the grown-up here. I am the mommy.

Oh, Lord, please give me some moments to refuel. Since I can't run away from my kids or responsibilities, You'll have to meet me here in this house. Remind me how special it is to be the one that they need.

Your presence renews me. These prayers restore me. Thank You for always being with me to breathe newness into a day that, too quickly, grew old. I love You.

AMEN.

And surely I am with you always,
to the very end of the age.

—Matthew 28:20

DRAWING NEAR

LORD,

Four sets of eyes follow my every move. I hear our baby mimic my inflections. I watch our sons imitate the silly faces I taught them. I see our oldest daughter, Taylor, shedding her dress-up clothes and becoming a young lady. I look at the way they walk and giggle and play and see that there is a striking resemblance to me. I am aware that little eyes now see, as through a microscope, all the good and bad that's inside me.

I yearn to be a better mother. I long to be the kind of mother that my children introduce with pride to their friends. I want to be the one they're glad to go home with.

Yet I know that improving and growing will only come from a deeper relationship with You. If I am walking close to You, my priorities will be godly. If I listen to You, I will speak to them from Your wisdom. If I study Your Word, I will have clear direction for my path and for theirs. Oh, I crave to be closer to You.

Lord, for my sake and for theirs, come near. Take hold of my life and never let go. Please do whatever it takes to make me into a mother of great strength and devotion. Give me a character that is worthy of reproduction. Make me better in Your arms than I would ever be on my own. Let me be a mighty woman of God.

I am filled with the presence of Your Spirit. I know that You are faithful to draw near. I need You, my Jesus.

AMEN.

Draw near to God and He will
draw near to you.

—James 4:8 NAS

DANNY'S GOT DOWN'S

LORD,

Danny is one of the sweetest babies I've ever held. His smile is pure and consuming. His spirit is already winsome. He is loving and cuddly. His parents say he's stolen their hearts. I'm not surprised; he steals the heart of everyone who knows him. Dear little Danny has Down's Syndrome.

Holding Danny fills me with all kinds of emotion. Absolute love for him. Absolute love for my babies. Gratefulness. Guilt. Joy. Sorrow. Hope. Deep, deep compassion. Danny could have just as easily been born to me. I don't have any idea why he wasn't.

His parents have to be the strongest people I've ever had the pleasure of knowing. There isn't a "pity me" bone in their bodies. They were sad to know that their baby won't have the life they'd planned; but they proclaim, without question, that he is the one for them. They say that Danny is their greatest blessing. They tell everyone that their lives would be empty without him—that he brings joy, laughter, and sunshine to their lives.

Still, Lord, I know there must be difficult days. Meet them there, in the midst of every struggle, and prove to them that You are more than sufficient. Overwhelm them with Your grace. Surround them with a safe harbor of family and friends.

Danny is Yours. He bears Your image. You are pleased with Your beloved son, and for a season, You have entrusted him to our friends. Abide in their home. Perfect Your power in their weakness. In the name of Christ, our amazing Savior and friend,

AMEN.

But he said to me, "My grace is sufficient for you, for my power is made perfect in weakness." Therefore I will boast all the more gladly about my weaknesses, so that Christ's power may rest on me.

—2 Corinthians 12:9

GOD DOES MORE

LORD,

When Paul and I pray, we believe that You hear. We are confident that You will answer. We know that You are faithful, but sometimes we waver. We have waited patiently on some days and impatiently on others. Sometimes it seemed like You were silent. There have been days when it felt like You were gone. We have cried out in our frustration, "Where are You, God?"

In the darkest days, through the places of struggle, we have come to know You more intimately. We have learned that You are always in control. We have learned that Your silence means, "Stand still and wait." We have yet to see Your plans unravel and fall apart. Your thoughts are so much greater than ours. You are very rarely early, but always on time.

You can never be persuaded to do less, when You have always intended to do more. Oh, God, thank You for always doing more. The birth of each one of our babies has brought us more joy than we could ever hope for or imagine. Our lofty dreams seem so feeble compared to the plan You are working out in our lives.

I want to shout it out so that all will hear, "If you trust in God . . . remain steadfast through the hard years . . . cry out on the lonely days . . . don't move when you're lost . . . and be faithful to pray, God will always, always, do more!" It's the truth of Scripture and the lesson of my life. To You be the glory in the church and in Christ Jesus to all generations forever and ever.

AMEN.

Now to him who is able to do immeasurably more than all we ask or imagine, according to his power that is at work within us, to him be the glory in the church and in Christ Jesus throughout all generations, for ever and ever! Amen.

—Ephesians 3:20–21

THE STORYTELLER

OH, LORD, MY GOD,

My grandmother was taken to the hospital last night. Intensive care. No diagnosis. Things don't sound very good. My heart aches with sadness. In real life, hard days always take me by surprise. I'm not ready to let go of her. I wanted my children to get the opportunity to love my grandmother, too.

My grandmother is a storyteller. She can remember every detail from the past eighty years. She only tells the stories that make her laugh, but almost everything makes her laugh. Yet she has taught each of us to love You and how to be reverent in Your presence.

After her boys were grown, my grandmother got her driver's license and "Ol' Blue." She'd often take all us grandchildren to Speedy Chef for ice cream, but while backing out, sometimes she'd scrape the mailbox at the end of the driveway with her fender. She'd act like she didn't notice, and we'd all giggle in the back seat. However, before we could go anywhere, she'd reach up over the sun visor and pull out her devotional. One of us would read the devotion and one of us would pray. She'd shout, "Amen," and off we'd be. I wonder how many angels You had to send to watch over her coming and going?

Lord, if You decide to bring her home, just get ready because Heaven won't ever be the same. You won't need a trumpet to announce her arrival. You'll see her from a long way off, hollering and dancing a jig. Our great loss would truly be Heaven's gain.

Put enough of her inside of me so that my babies will be able to know her. I love her.

AMEN.

Love the LORD your God with all your heart and with all your soul and with all your strength. These commandments that I give you today are to be upon your hearts. Impress them on your children. Talk about them when you sit at home and when you walk along the road, when you lie down and when you get up.

—Deuteronomy 6:5–7

KEEPSAKES

LORD,

There are so many things to cherish:

A tiny ID bracelet.

A newborn hospital cap and booties.

The newspaper from the day of her birth.

A pink bubble gum cigar.

Her homecoming dress.

Two tiny ink footprints on paper.

A lock of hair tied with a ribbon of pink.

That first squinty-eyed picture.

The gifts her brothers and sister presented.

A white crocheted blanket.

A tiny pink Bible.

These are my baby's keepsakes. To look at them is precious. To touch them is to hold my newborn again. Thank You for little treasures that remind me of that wonderful day she was born. For the sake of our memories, we keep holding onto the reminders . . . souvenirs for our soul.

Thank You, Jesus.

AMEN.

But Mary treasured up all these things
and pondered them in her heart.

—Luke 2:19

A FAIRLY FUNCTIONAL FAMILY

LORD,

With one finger on the remote control, I can turn on the TV and find story after story of children from dysfunctional families. Bold headlines proclaim that our homes are not okay. A high percentage of marriages now end in divorce. What used to be the institution of family is crumbling from the inside out.

These are frightening days for parents! I'd be foolish to think our family is immune. But we want to raise children who won't need therapy. We want a fairly functional family. Can we have a happy home with happy children? Can we remain stable while the world goes wild? Can Paul and I stay in love for a lifetime? I'm sure that we can't do anything without You. We must anchor ourselves to the Lord God Almighty.

The enemies of our society threaten to sneak in and plunder our homes. The family is now an unwitting target for sin's invasion and conquest. The guard has not diligently kept his watch. The residents are sleeping. The attackers can easily creep in.

Dear Father, please build a spiritual moat around our lives. Protect us from the evil that lurks. Give us enough wisdom to know when to lower the drawbridge and when to keep the gates securely fastened. You are our only hope. You are the only sure thing we can count on. You alone provide the stamina we need to persevere. God, protect the precious treasures You have given us. Let us lead our children in paths of righteousness all the days of our lives. In the blessed name of Jesus,

AMEN.

Fathers, do not exasperate your children;
instead, bring them up in the training
and instruction of the Lord.

—Ephesians 6:4

NINETY-FIFTH PERCENTILE

LORD,

Anna Grace's weight and height now place her in the ninety-fifth percentile on the growth charts. Never before have we had such a big baby! I guess that if we had ten, none of them would be exactly the same. That must be the key to this whole thing. Extra big or average-sized, they are all individuals to be loved. I must value their differences as much as I love their similarities.

She is exactly the person You created. She reflects the image of our family in her own distinct and unique ways. She has blue eyes like Grayson, light brown hair that looks a lot like Taylor's, and the same infectious smile that You gave William. She definitely belongs with our tribe, but lately she's been showing us that she's more different than she is the same.

I must accept the fact that, even though we are mother and daughter, we will surely be different in many ways. Her future is not mine to live. I cannot force her to share my interests. I risk the chance of wounding her spirit. I want to look for her gifts and nurture them. I want to see her uniqueness and applaud it. I want to be the mother and let her be the daughter.

Lord, You knew Anna Grace before You formed her. You have set her apart for a special work. May we bless her as our daughter and give her the freedom to be the person You intend for her to be. By Your grace, she will always remain distinctly Yours.

AMEN.

Before I formed you in the womb I knew you,
before you were born I set you apart.

—Jeremiah 1:5

195

NEW PRIORITIES

OH, LORD,

Boy, have things changed around here. I mean really changed. I vaguely remember the days I couldn't run to the store before my hair and make-up were perfectly done. I would put on clean clothes because of a dot of ketchup. My life was color-coordinated and wrinkle-free, seamless to the beholder, and incredibly hard to maintain.

I'm embarrassed to think about all the time I wasted on things that don't really matter. I worked hard at holding onto a standard of ridiculous priorities. I sacrificed authenticity for appearances. I missed out on some great living while I was pretending. Thankfully, new babies bring new priorities. Gone are those self-possessed days (forcefully stripped from me is more like it). But I am glad to lose that layer of plastic.

Thank You for this new baby and the real life she brings to our home. Teach our family how to live purely in these days. Interruptible. Honest. Unpretentious. Simple. Real. Very real. Make sure that I maintain the most important things, the things that matter for eternity, at the top of my "to do" list. Help me stop chasing after the trivial. Instead, may I capture the timeless.

Lord, let us pass these new priorities down to our children. May they live free from the bondage of meaningless pursuits. May they strive for significance and yearn for the spiritually substantial. Grant us enough wisdom to recognize what is important. Thank You for the baby that forces us to let go of the old and run after new (and better) priorities. In Jesus' name,

AMEN.

But seek first his kingdom and his righteousness,
and all these things will be given
to you as well.

—Matthew 6:33

AND SHE GROWS

LORD,

Everyone said it would happen. I just listened and nodded like I knew what they meant. "Anna Grace will be grown before you know it," they proclaimed.

I know their words are true. Our other three children have grown up too fast. But this time my heart aches a little deeper. We believe that our quiver is full. And so, she is the baby of my babies.

Everything's happening so fast—too fast. I feel like we've been catapulted by a time machine. Where have eight months gone? They flew by like mere moments. Now she is trying to crawl. She can almost sit up. She loves table food, and she sips juice from a cup. I want her to do those things. But then again, I don't. It is bittersweet to watch her grow.

I want to hold onto that baby I brought home from the hospital. The one who couldn't straighten her back or try to get down. I want to cuddle and rock her for at least another twenty years. And so it goes. . . . For the rest of her life, she will continue to grow up and move on. The rest of my life I will fight my yearnings to hold her back.

I joke with Grayson and Taylor, saying, "You're not allowed to grow up." I pretend to cry when they've grown a little taller. I pretend to whine when they need bigger clothes. Grayson says, "It's okay, Mommy; I promise I'll always be your baby." Oh, thank You, God, that they will always be my babies. I am blessed.

AMEN.

And Jesus grew in wisdom and stature,
and in favor with God and men.

—Luke 2:52

A PLACE OF GRACE

LORD,

Despite ten and a half years of marriage, in some ways, it still feels like Paul and I have only just begun. Yes, our family is complete. Our house is full. We look forward to the rest of our lives. But we don't want to just wander through the decades of our lives. We want our days to have purpose and meaning. What principles should guide us and our family? If we could write a mission statement and hang it over our door, what would You want it to say? Perhaps it should read something like this:

Welcome to this place of grace.
We, the people who live here, love one
    another and love Jesus.

Our home is a haven, a refuge of acceptance
and forgiveness and love.
We believe that we are divinely appointed to
be a family.
We will walk together through every valley.
We will rejoice together from every mountain.
We will pursue godliness.
We will look for each other's giftedness,
and encourage one another toward
significance.
We will live pure lives.
We will pray.
We will worship.
We will seek God first in all things.
We believe it is better to laugh and cry
together, than to accomplish great feats
all alone.
We are stronger because we are family.
To God be the glory for the great things He
has done.
Hallelujah.

AMEN.

I urge you to live a life worthy of the calling
you have received. Be completely humble and
gentle; be patient, bearing with one another in
love. Make every effort to keep the unity of
the Spirit through the bond of peace.

—Ephesians 4:1–3

THE BLESSING

LORD,

Bless my sweet darling, Anna Grace. Hold her securely in Your strong hands of mercy. Protect her. Defend her. Send a myriad of angels to guard every step she takes. Strengthen her body. Keep sickness away. We entrust our priceless treasure to You for safekeeping.

May she come to know You intimately as her personal Savior. May she always find rest in Your great arms of love. May Your awesome works as Almighty God overwhelm her. May she abide always in her Redeemer's arms of grace. May she serve You as Lord. May she trust You as Friend. Give her an unswerving faith and an unquenchable thirst for You this side of Heaven.

Let her grow in great wisdom and honor. Give her an inquisitive mind and a hunger for knowledge. Endow her with common sense and the ability to apply all that her mind possesses. Give her an unfailing sense of what is right. May she be a woman of integrity. A woman of principle. A woman of purity. Honest. Diligent. Compelling. Generous. Kind. Good. May she be a virtuous woman of God.

Give her a wonderful family. A marvelous man to love and adore for a lifetime. Children who will rise up and call her blessed. Allow her enough struggles to grow character. Bestow on her the rewards of perseverance. May she preserve the legacy of our family and pursue holiness all the days of her life.

We invoke Your blessing for this precious baby in the name of the Father, the Son, and the Holy Spirit. May You receive all the glory and honor both now and forever.

AMEN.

The LORD bless you and keep you; the LORD make his face shine upon you and be gracious to you; the LORD turn his face toward you and give you peace.

—Numbers 6:24–26

And God is able to make all grace abound to you, so that in all things at all times, having all that you need, you will abound in every good work.

—2 Corinthians 9:8

Scripture Index

ABOUT THE AUTHOR

Angela Thomas Guffey is a graduate of The University of North Carolina at Chapel Hill, and Dallas Theological Seminary. She and her husband, Paul, live in Tennessee where she is a stay-at-home mom to their four children.

Angela teaches a women's Bible study and is a frequent speaker at women's retreats, conferences, and seminars. *Prayers for New Mothers* was written after the birth of her fourth child. She also wrote *Prayers for Expectant Mothers* during her fourth pregnancy.

You can write to Angela via the Internet at:
Angela@worshiphim.com

Additional copies of this book
are available from
your local bookstore.

Also by Angela Thomas Guffey:

Prayers for Expectant Mothers

If you have enjoyed this book, or if it has impacted
your life, we would like to hear from you.

Please contact us at:

Honor Books
Department E
P.O. Box 55388
Tulsa, Oklahoma 74155
Or by e-mail at info@honorbooks.com

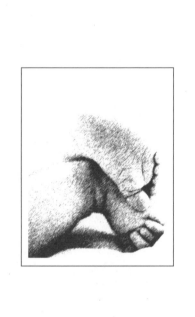